THE SEXUAL RIGHTS
OF ADOLESCENTS
Competence, Vulnerability,
and Parental Control

THE SEXUAL RIGHTS OF ADOLESCENTS

Competence, Vulnerability, and Parental Control

Hyman Rodman
Susan H. Lewis
Saralyn B. Griffith

COLUMBIA UNIVERSITY PRESS
NEW YORK   1984

Library of Congress Cataloging in Publication Data

Rodman, Hyman.
The sexual rights of adolescents.

Bibliography: p.
Includes index.
1. Youth—United States—Sexual behavior.
2. Children—Legal status, laws, etc.—United States.
3. Parent and child—United States.   4. Contraception—
United States.   5. Abortion services—United States.
6. Youth—Sexual behavior—Government policy—United
States.   I. Lewis, Susan H.   II. Griffith, Saralyn B.
III. Title.   [DNLM: 1. Sex behavior—In adolescence.
2. Parent-child relations.   3. Human rights.
4. Contraception—In adolescence.   5. Abortion—In
adolescence.   WS 462 R693s]
HQ27.R624   1984   306.8′74   83-14440
ISBN 0-231-04916-1

Columbia University Press
New York   Guildford, Surrey
Copyright © 1984 Columbia University Press
All rights reserved

Printed in the United States of America

Clothbound editions of Columbia University Press Books are Smyth-
sewn and printed on permanent and durable acid-free paper

Contents

Preface

Young children need their parents' help in making decisions. As they grow older, they are able to make many decisions on their own. Certain decisions are both important and controversial. To have sexual intercourse? To use contraceptives? If pregnant, to have an abortion? We need to know whether adolescents are competent to make these decisions, or whether they are vulnerable and require parental guidance. Difficult policy judgments are currently being made about adolescents' competence and vulnerability. Should they have the right to live where they please, to marry, to make legal contracts, and to obtain medical care without parental consent? Or should consent be required in order to protect minors and to preserve parental authority?

In the United States, the major resolutions to these difficult questions are being worked out by the courts as they decide cases of conflict between the wishes of adolescents and the prerogatives of parents. The first goal of this book is to spell out these policy resolutions, especially in the area of adolescents' sexual rights. Although sexual rights can include freedom to engage in various forms of sexual behavior, to buy pornographic materials, to obtain medical care and counseling for a variety of sex-related health needs, and to obtain sexual information and education, our major focus is on minors' access to contraception and abortion services. The question of minors' access to contraception and abortion are among the most difficult and controversial social policy issues we face. What decisions and actions can minors legally carry out on their own? When do they have to get their parents' consent, or to involve their parents in some other way? What role does the state play in deciding such questions? Legislatures and courts continue to make difficult decisions about minors' rights and parental involvement, and we can expect to see many more decisions in the coming years.

Providing useful information to policymakers who are considering these issues is another focus of this book. We will review the available social science information about minors' competence to make important decisions, and the available information on minors' contraception and abortion behavior and decisions. This will make it possible to examine whether minors' legal rights are in harmony with our knowledge about their social and psychological competence. It will also make it possible to explore how minors' decision making involves parents and other adults, and whether this suggests policy directions. We recognize that the research data are limited and that values loom large over these policy issues. Nevertheless we believe that an approach that combines legal and social science data can contribute to the policymaking process.

An additional objective of the book, albeit an indirect objective, is to illuminate the general contours of parent-child relationships in the United States. By focusing on cases in which parent-child relationships do not go smoothly, in which conflicts among parents, adolescents, and states enter the courtroom, we may shed indirect light on the more mundane aspects of the parent-child tie. Almost all parent-child interaction takes place outside the courts, and almost all conflicts are handled privately within each family. As long as the actions of parents and children fall within the range of what is normative or tolerable, there is no problem. But when actions go beyond that range, the state may intervene. Or when difficult policy questions emerge about the conflicting rights of children, parents, and the state, the courts may be asked to intervene. Our focus on the boundary between what is normal and what is extraordinary can therefore provide a unique position from which to understand the relationship between parents and children.

We have presented sufficient information on the legal, social, and psychological aspects of adolescents' sexual rights so that readers can come to their own conclusions about desirable social policies. Using the background information ourselves, we offer three realistic policy recommendations, providing reasons and supporting evidence for each one. Partisans in the bitter family planning debate may not agree with us, but we think that a substantial majority of the population would agree, and we hope that our recommendations will help chart social policies for the future.

Acknowledgments

W E could not have completed this book without the support and assistance of many individuals and organizations. The first author had a year's research leave from the University of North Carolina at Greensboro (UNC-G) and spent it as a guest scholar at the Brookings Institution. A substantial portion of the book was written during that year, and we are thankful to both UNC-G and Brookings.

We appreciate the grant support from the William T. Grant Foundation to the Family Research Center at UNC-G. These funds helped to move the project forward at critical times.

We also express our appreciation to—

• the library staff of UNC-G, Brookings Institution, and Duke University Law Library;

• Bates Buckner, Betty Harris, Holly Hanna, and Martha Stewart for research assistance;

• Patty Herring, Ann Smith, and Dorrence Stewart for typing assistance;

• Karin Gleiter for copyediting assistance.

We are grateful——

• for moral support and encouragement, to Garrett Lange, J. Allen Watson, and Kelley Griffith at UNC-G; Martha Derthick and Gilbert Steiner at the Brookings Institution; Joan McQuary, John Moore, and Charles Webel at Columbia University Press; and to Douglas Besharov and Bates Buckner;

• for critically constructive readings of earlier versions of the manuscript, to Douglas Besharov, Patricia Donovan, Asta Kenney, Sylvia Law, and John Scanzoni.

Many others, too numerous to mention, provided help with specific questions that came up; we thank them all for their invaluable assistance.

Responsibility for the book rests solely with the authors. None of the views expressed in the book should be attributed to any of the individuals or organizations mentioned above.

THE SEXUAL RIGHTS
OF ADOLESCENTS
Competence, Vulnerability,
and Parental Control

Introduction

Family Quandaries

Is the American family breaking apart? Are parents losing authority and control over their children? Is the U.S. Supreme Court giving teenagers more rights than they can competently handle? Is the Court destroying parental authority and family harmony by the drift of its decisions?

These questions are being asked by the mass media and by increasing numbers of Americans. They reflect anxiety about whether our society faces a moral crisis—with government, the professions, business, and labor all contributing to the decline of the country's moral fiber. This anxiety centers especially upon the family, because by tradition we see families as the basic units of society, the private factories in which the country's moral fiber is spun. As a result, public worries about the major institutions of society often come to focus with special intensity on the family.

We therefore confront one of the many problems that our national fetish with morality creates for us. At one and the same time the family is the source of support, nurturance, and love, protecting its members from the onslaughts of the cruel world—and it is the source of cruelty and violence because it is too weak and too isolated to control its members or teach them respect, sacrifice, and morality.

It is not altogether surprising that the family is seen as both savior and satan. Our most intense experiences—positive and negative, love and hatred—occur within the privacy of the family. We start our lives within families, and our parents are of supreme importance during the early years of our childhood. In the privacy of the family parents have enormous power and influence. Thus, when social scientists seek a universal definition of the family, they zero in on the parent-child relationship. The family is frequently defined as the group which provides nurturance and training to children, enabling society to survive from generation to generation. In our culture the family is the central social institution by which each generation transmits a social and moral code to the next generation. As a result, when we fear that the code is not working well, we often make the family the scapegoat for our frustrations.

This propels our national thinking into a series of contradictions. If the family is weak and unable to instill morality in its children, we must do something to help it. So we create programs to provide day care services for children or training in citizenship and sex education. But our social and moral problems do not miraculously disappear, and our families still face many difficulties. We then criticize the state for infringing upon the family's private domain through such programs as sex education for school-age children. No wonder the family is in trouble, we say—the state is interfering with it and undercutting parents' authority and moral values. Of course, the same people do not argue all of these propositions at the same time. But all of them are argued, all of them are aired by the mass media, all of them are given some credence by large segments of the population. Is it any wonder that our national debates shed more heat than light? That we spin around in circles with a marvelous moral frenzy, but get only as far as a random walk or erratic spin will take us?

The public and the mass media are not alone in engaging in circular debates about the family. Social scientists also enter the whirlpool. They do so with some advantages: they have facts at their fingertips, they have an historical perspective on the problem, and they have access to alternative interpretations. Nevertheless, they too spin their circular webs, though in more sophisticated patterns. Christopher Lasch (1975), for example, argues that the family is no longer a "haven in a heartless world," but that it has been torn asunder and rendered incompetent by the intrusions of helping professionals and government bureaucrats. Mary Jo Bane (1976), however, presents demographic facts to support her position that the family is "here to stay" and is doing its job rather well. Some social scientists, writing from a feminist perspective, decry society's failure to value the work women do in the home, and deplore women's disproportionate burden of housework and child care. But Urie Bronfenbrenner (1976, 1977a, 1977b), a peripatetic critic of the lack of time and attention that mothers (and fathers) devote to their children, fears that these feminist scruples jeopardize children's social and emotional development.

Whom are we to believe? How is it that social scientists disagree? Values are obviously involved, both in the social scientists' and in the public's interpretations of our social condition. This is not surprising since values are also involved in more technical areas, where scientists as well as policymakers disagree about the safety of nuclear reactors, drugs, or food additives. Clashing values, contrasting interpretations of facts, and diametrically opposed calls to partisan action are typical of a morally and emotionally charged area like the family—and of related topics like sexual behavior, family planning, and abortion.

Since the pervasive view of the family is pessimistic, it is no wonder that Lasch's and Bronfenbrenner's ominous accounts are more popular than the sanguine interpretations. Pessimism is also supported by the "bad news" syndrome of the mass media, which soak up and spin out doomsday bulletins because of their inherent drama.

It is impossible fully to resolve these national concerns about the family's decay or the family's strength, because the facts do not speak for themselves. They are filtered through our past experiences and interpreted in the mottled light of our values. As a result accounts of "what is happening to the family" can be informative and even brilliant, but they cannot definitively answer our questions. The answers take a different shape and different shades of meaning according to the social and moral context in which we find ourselves.

Social class, gender, race, age, and political orientation are some of the contextual filters through which we perceive families and parent-child relationships. But social issues and social movements also affect our ideas about the family. Concerns about a "sexual revolution" (especially the sexual behavior of adolescents) and about rising divorce rates are deeply felt. The omnipresent television set, spewing forth sex, violence, and frivolous commercials, profoundly affects the family and our ideas about the family. Finally, contemporary developments like the women's movement are part of the social context within which our ideologies and policies about the family are formed.

Americans create their own quandaries to wrestle with. We are distressed by the frequency of family violence, but wary of the state's "intrusive" attempts to protect family members. We are unwilling to treat juveniles as criminals, yet capable only of creating a system of juvenile justice that "benignly" punishes them for noncriminal offenses. We are upset by insidious junk food commercials directed at children on television and yet hesitant to restrict such commercials. We are distressed by parents who cannot adequately raise their children, but fearful of turning professionals loose to "support" the family. We are upset by rampant individualism and by the growth of alternatives (cohabitation, divorce, abortion, voluntary childlessness), yet we recognize that this involves individual freedom and choice in the best democratic tradition.

The quandary we face because of our commitment to family privacy is most intractable of all (cf. Steiner 1976, 1981). We cherish individual and family privacy; parental authority is strongly supported; the privacy and sanctity of the home are enshrined in our Constitution. Yet we recognize that under the cloak of privacy atrocities may occur. The family that is free to pursue its private interests, without interference from the state, is also free to treat its members (especially, but not only, its children) in an oppressive manner. To protect family members from oppression the state must be able to intervene. The balance necessary to protect both the family's privacy and individual members from the family's oppression is delicate and difficult. As Clarke-Stewart says, "Our greatest challenge may be to increase public responsibility for children without destroying the sanctity or privacy of the family or the decision-making power of parents" (1977:116).

Let us examine, in more detail, how the family privacy quandary is reflected in the relationship between parent and child. We will look successively at the children's rights movement, at troubling questions about parental competence, at the pervasiveness of family violence, and at "divorces" between parents and children.

CHILDREN'S RIGHTS MOVEMENT

The children's rights movement reflects a strong American concern with individual rights. Some see it as a natural outgrowth of the civil rights movement and the women's movement, which raised issues that are crisp and clear. There is no rational basis for withholding equal rights from blacks, Hispanics, or women. But "equal rights" for children is an issue that is not at all clear. Child advocates have provocatively asked: Do children have the right to pursue sexually pleasurable lives, including intercourse with adults? Do children have the right to "divorce" and live apart from their parents (Farson 1974; Constantine 1977; McMurty 1979–80; cf. *Time* 1981a)? Such suggestions add fuel to the fiery debates about child and family policy endemic to the United States. As Baumrind (1978b) notes, the zeal of some child advocates can lead them to forget the fundamental differences between children and adults (cf. Finkelhor 1979).

When aggressive advocates of equal rights for children are asked: "Beginning when? At birth? At the age of two? Five?" they have difficulty in responding. There are biological limits to what infants and children can do. Children need help and protection, and they need to learn many things before they can competently assume adult rights and responsibilities.

A few children's advocates, however, insist on total liberation for children. They are not prepared to accept any limits, not even those justified by the presumed incapacity of children. Children are treated like slaves, they argue, and radical changes are needed to free them from ruthless and arbitrary adult control (McMurty 1979–80).

Other advocates, more moderate, want children to have legal rights to do and decide much earlier than is now the case. They want children to be tested for their competence to pursue activities that are now arbitrarily prohibited on account of age. Driving a car is an example. There is nothing magically capacitating about becoming 15 or 16 years of age. Some 16-year-olds are not competent and do not pass their driving tests. But some adults do not pass either. Why shouldn't a 13-year-old be permitted to take the same test, and be judged on performance (cf. Lee 1982)? Such questions about the competence of children and adolescents lie at the core of this book, and we shall return to them again.

The issue of children's rights does not have to be framed in terms of whether children can make decisions entirely on their own. Should children be consulted about certain decisions that affect their lives? Informally, of course, children are regularly consulted about and involved in family decisions, although the extent to which this is done varies greatly among families. But should children legally be entitled to have a voice in custody decisions or in decisions about their treatment for physical or mental illness? Once again the answers to such questions revolve around children's age and children's competence; they also depend upon the nature of the decision, and upon the risks and gains that the decision holds for the child (Gaylin 1982). Regardless of whether one is inclined to grant children much or little involvement in such decisions, there is no disagreement about the proposition that older and more competent children are better able to play a role in such decisions.

THE COMPETENCE OF PARENTS

Many parents do a poor job of raising their children. Some subject their children to serious physical abuse or neglect. Is there some way of raising the level of parental competence? Do we need "societal mechanisms" to detect parental incompetence and to protect children? (Caldwell 1980)

People must pass a test to demonstrate competence in driving a car before being licensed to drive. Why should we not test people's competence before we permit them to marry or to have children? These activities are at least as important as driving, and a reasonable case can be made for requiring such tests. Testing would emphasize the importance of marriage and parenthood and would help assure that those undertaking them have the wisdom and competence to carry them out.

At present the legal requirements for marriage are minimal. People of proper age, free of venereal disease, and competent to know what they are doing, can marry. A simple medical test determines if a person is free of venereal disease. But there is no specific test to determine his or her competence to marry. Only those who are grossly incompetent, such as the severely retarded, are ruled out by this requirement. It is assumed that individuals who can apply for a license to marry and appear for the marriage ceremony are competent to marry. And once married—in fact, regardless of marital status—they are free to have children.

It is probably possible to devise a test that, if used as a screening device, would raise the level of parental competence and reduce the level of child abuse and neglect. Proposals for such testing, however, are currently unrealistic, and we do not advocate or support such tests. The risk of bias in the testing procedure should give us pause: Are we socially, politically, and ethically ready to deny such basic human rights as marriage or parenthood to individuals who "fail" a competency test? Are we ready to insist upon sterilization for those who fail the parenting test? Fortunately, the constitutional barrier that limits the state's right to intervene in such intimate decisions is virtually insurmountable.

The issue of parental competence also arises in areas where it is more difficult to know what to do. In individual cases of child abuse or neglect, is the situation serious enough for the state to intervene, and perhaps remove the child from the care of its parents? Once the child is removed, should courts condition the child's return on the parents' enrolling in a training program to improve their effectiveness as parents? Should the public schools teach children sex education, on the grounds that parents do not or can not? Or should the state, the courts, and the public schools leave families alone?

These are not idle questions. Decisions are being made every day that presuppose answers to them. On sex education, for example, debate is still raging around the country. Some organizations are fighting sex education programs on the grounds that they are immoral, irreligious, and subversive of parental authority and values. Several members of the Reagan administration have said that sex education is a parental responsibility and has no place in the public schools. One of the continuing problems in many communities—although only rarely raised as a problem—is the competence of sex education teachers. It may be true that most parents are not competent to teach sex education; unfortunately most teachers are not competent either.

One hopeful sign is the voluntary interest by many parents in improving their competence through programs of parent education. The field of parent education, with a growing number of diverse practitioners, is attempting to meet the needs of parents, and it is doing so with at least some indications of success (Harman and Brim 1980).

FAMILY VIOLENCE

Child abuse has been a topic of serious research and clinical concern for about twenty years, wife battering for ten years. The poignant nature of most incidents of family violence keeps the topic in the forefront of the news in the United States. There are alarmists who see family violence as symptomatic of the final throes of the family's death, and hold that the amount and severity of family violence are increasing. Actually, we do not know whether family violence is rising or falling. Unlike marriage, birth, and divorce statistics, statistics on family violence have not been kept; the existing data are spongy because collecting data on such an emotionally charged topic is extremely difficult. Murray Straus and his colleagues (1980), who have carried out major research on the topic, speculate that the figures they have collected, showing a great deal of family violence, represent only half the true incidence. They also suggest that the current rate of family violence is about the same as in the past, or perhaps a bit lower than in the past.

One can make a rather good case for a declining rate of family violence. This is because there has been a recent decrease in its long-standing cultural support. As many have pointed out, our television programs, our folklore, our jokes, and even our laws have encouraged or tolerated a good deal of violence within the family. Men still joke about beating their wives; women may equate a beating with a demonstration of love and concern; advertisements have used the theme, as in Finnair's short-lived explanation of how a Finnish man discovered the sauna: "He locked his wife in the smokehouse, set it on fire, beat her with birch leaves, and discovered she loved it."

It is only in very recent years that the women's movement has organized a counteroffensive to the often unthinking support and acceptance of family violence. As a result, at least over the short term, there is growing concern about family violence, a growing effort to expose it and to help the victims, and a rising number of organizations and laws to cope with the problem. This could produce a rise in the available figures on family violence, but perhaps also a drop in its actual incidence.

Our major concern, however, is not with the rate of family violence but with the relationship among parent, child, and state. The quandary about family privacy embraces the problem of family violence. Although a great deal of conflict is accommodated and absorbed within the everyday life of the family, as is a considerable amount of emotional neglect and physical violence, beyond a certain level of neglect and violence there is a social consensus to help the victim and perhaps to punish the perpetrator. But who should actually do so? Since agencies of the state are involved, the "delicate balance" issue is again raised: how to assure the family's privacy while simultaneously providing protection to helpless or dependent members of a family suffering neglect or abuse. A further vexing question is posed by Besharov (1982): If the state contemplates the child's involuntary removal from the family, does it have better alternatives for the child's care?

PARENT-CHILD DIVORCE

A latent issue, but one that will gradually generate greater public concern, is the strength and permanence of the tie between parents and children. Should parents be able to "divorce" their children, or children their parents? Although there are virtually no legal parent-child divorces in the United States, there are several informal practices that are tantamount to divorce. Some parents and some children run away from home; separation takes place, if not divorce. Some parents take their children to court as incorrigible; in many of these cases the state takes the children off the parents' hands. Because of charges of neglect or abuse the state sometimes intervenes and removes children from their homes. In all these instances the tie between parent and child is largely severed, and in effect there is an informal parent-child divorce. In a few cases, where the parents' rights are involuntarily terminated or voluntarily relinquished, in order to free a child for adoption, we can speak of a legal parent-child divorce.

These divorces take place under extraordinary conditions and serve as a safety valve to relieve the pressure of the relationship. (The unmarried woman who releases her child for adoption is perhaps avoiding later pressure.) Except for the termination of parental rights in legal adoption procedures, however, the legal status of parent-child divorce is tenuous, and the freedom to effect a divorce is limited. The minor who "divorces" his parents by running away can be charged as a runaway and brought back by force. If he continues to run away, he can be charged with incorrigibility and incarcerated. It is a serious limitation of a child's freedom to "divorce" his parents that the "divorce" is subject to parental consent and state intervention. Many parents accept a child's wish to leave; some are relieved by or have even encouraged it. Nevertheless, many minors confront a Catch-22 situation. Because of serious conflicts they want to leave their parents, but their ability to do so depends upon their parents' willingness to accept the separation.

The exceptional case of Walter Polovchak, who ran away from his parents when they decided to leave the United States and return to the Soviet Union, illustrates the issue of parent-child divorce and how it overlaps the topic of children's rights. In 1980, when Walter was 12 years old, he received asylum in the United States under federal law. Under Illinois state law the circuit court held that he was incorrigible, beyond his parents' control, and in need of state supervision; this unusual ruling was reversed by the Illinois Supreme Court in 1983 (FLR 1983). If state law alone were involved, Walter would be released to his parents' custody if they return to the United States, but federal litigation regarding his asylum in the United States is still pending. While parental custody would not ordinarily be denied in similar circumstances, political undercurrents have delayed a final decision in the case. Meanwhile, the parents' chances of winning custody diminish with time as Walter approaches the age of maturity.

Some have raised an almost unthinkable question: should we make it much easier for parents to legally divorce their children, and for children to legally divorce their parents? In some legal jurisdictions a child who is mature or who is independent can gain legal emancipation in order to be treated as an adult and to live apart from his or her parents. Such separations can and do solve some disputes between parents and children, and do not create great strains in the American legal system. A more permissive legal approach to make separation or divorce easier at either the child's or parents' behest, however, would not be in harmony with current laws or values.

PART ONE

THE LEGAL BACKGROUND

1

The Legal View of the Parent-Child Relationship

PARENT-CHILD divorce is as unthinkable to some people today as husband-wife divorce was for most people in the fifteenth century. And there are some parallels in the thought that underlies the resistance to each idea. Both relationships have been thought by some to originate with God, and for that reason to be inseverable. The dependent party in the relationship—the wife or the child—has been viewed as wholly incompetent, at least in the legal sense, and therefore as unable to function in society on his own. A wife's incompetence resulted from the loss of her individual legal identity when she married: under the doctrine of "femme coverte" she lost the capacity to contract and manage her own affairs. Unfortunately for the child, the idea that he is a helpless, ignorant incompetent arises from the impression he makes at his first entrance into the world. "The infant lies in utter want and helplessness," says Lucretius and, as Dickens warns, "first impressions . . . often go a long way."

Some would say that this initial view of the minor as incompetent and dependent stays with him well beyond his arriving at true competence and independence. A clue to the legal perspective on the competence of minors is the legal terminology applied to them: the law continues to call minors "infants" until they reach majority. The assumption that minors are helpless, ignorant, incompetent, and totally dependent appears to underlie most laws concerning children.

The child being totally dependent and helpless, the parent must be correspondingly powerful and controlling, and the concept of a parent's total power over his child permeates the legal view of the parent-child relationship. Legal deference to parental authority is reinforced by society's failure to find satisfactory substitutes for parents. No persons or groups are nearly so efficient, reliable, and affordable as are parents at providing for these members of society who require so much care. Parents are essentially indispensable in nurturing their children, and it is apparent that this reality is an assumption underlying the various legal doctrines addressing the parent-child relationship.

"PARENTAL PREROGATIVE" AND "FAMILY AUTONOMY"

The starting point for a review of the laws on parents and children is the "doctrine of parental prerogative." It derives from the well established legal tradition that parents have rightful power and authority over their children. One of the best early statements of the doctrine and the reasoning behind it is found in Blackstone:

> The *power* of parents over their children is derived from . . . their duty; this authority being given them, partly to enable the parent more effectually to perform his duty, and partly as a recompence for his care and trouble in the faithful discharge of it. . . . The ancient Roman laws gave the father a power of life and death over his children; upon this principle, that he who gave had also the power of taking away. . . . [S]ubsequent constitutions [have] maintained to the last a very large and absolute authority. . . .
>
> The power of a parent by our English laws is much more moderate; but still sufficient to keep the child in order and obedience. He may lawfully correct his child, being under age, in a reasonable manner; for this is the benefit of his education. . . . The legal power of a father . . . over the persons of his children ceases at the age of twenty-one: for they are then enfranchised by arriving at years of discretion, or that point which the law has established (as some must necessarily be established) when the em-

pire of the father, or other guardian, gives place to the empire of reason. (1765: 440–441)

The principle of parental control has been carried over from English to American case law as the "rule of parental control and authority." Most references to it appear in cases in which the question of parental control *per se* is not even at issue, for it is rare to find a case in which the issue of a direct conflict between a parent's wishes and those of his child is raised. Indeed, the "rule" is so embedded in the system as effectively to preclude a minor's seeking judicial redress in a conflict with his parents over discipline. Were he to pursue such judicial interference, he would learn that his parents' authority over him during minority is not subject to judicial review unless his life is endangered, or there are legal grounds for "terminating the parent-child relationship."

So rare is it for a court to intevene in a parent-child relationship that when a court purports to do so, the matter becomes sensational. The celebrated case of Walter Polovchak, the 12-year-old boy who ran away from home in 1980 to avoid returning to the Soviet Union with his parents, illustrates this point (see also *In the Matter of the Welfare of L.A.G.*, 1972). There are, of course, cases in which courts do interfere to save the life or health of the child, but short of a life-endangering situation the general approach is clearly established: as long as there are no legal grounds (abuse, neglect, abandonment, divorce) for altering or terminating the legally defined parent-child relationship, the court will not interfere and will not substitute its judgment for that of the parent. Implicit in this approach is the assumption that the parent can be entrusted with custody of the child and that the various daily decisions concerning the child can also be entrusted absolutely to the parent, without the necessity of state interference or supervision. (For other discussions of the competing and coinciding interests of childen, parents, and the state the reader is referred to ABA 1977, Stier 1978, Mnookin 1978a, CRS 1979, IJA 1980, Steinfels 1981, and Besharov 1982.)

Judicial deference to the "doctrine of parental prerogative" in parent-child disputes is closely related to the "doctrine of family autonomy." Just as the courts decline to interfere with most parental decisions and actions, so they also refuse to interfere in mother-father disputes about their children. A well-known Alabama case, *Kilgrow vs. Kilgrow,* illustrates this point. The dispute involved a family in which the parents strenuously disagreed over where to send their daughter to school. When the mother interfered with the father's attempt to take the daughter to the school of his choice, the father sued for an injunction against his wife to prevent such interference. The dispute reached the Supreme Court of Alabama, and the court refused to interfere, citing the "natural power and obligation . . . of parenthood" as the guiding principle:

The inherent jurisdiction of courts of equity over an infant is a matter of necessity, coming into exercise only where there has been a failure of that natural power and obligation which is the province of parenthood. It is a jurisdiction assumed by the courts only when it is forfeited by a natural custodian incident to a broken home or neglect, or as a result of a natural custodian's unfitness or death. It is only for a compelling reason that a parent is deprived of the custody of his or her child. . . . We do not think a court of equity should undertake to settle a dispute between parents as to what is best for their minor child when there is no question concerning the child's custody.

Again, in a similar case arising in New York, *People ex rel. Sisson vs. Sisson,* the New York Supreme Court declared:

Disputes between parents when it [sic] doesn't involve anything immoral or harmful to the welfare of the child is [sic] beyond the reach of the law. The vast majority of matters concerning the upbringing of children must be left to the conscience, patience and self-restraint of father and mother. No end of difficulties would arise should judges try to tell parents how to bring up their children.

Cases like *Kilgrow* and *Sisson* clearly illustrate the court's traditional refusal to interfere with or become involved in parental judgments on behalf of children. But this hands-off approach by the courts stands in sharp contrast to their attitude when faced with a request from a parent who is failing in efforts to discipline his child. In such a case, the state is deemed to have an interest in supporting a parent's effort to control his child, an interest expressed in the statutes creating the so-called status offenses.

A status offense is conduct that is illegal only because it is engaged in by a minor, and the breakdown of parental authority is usually implicit in such a situation. Many states treat status offenses in their criminal justice systems. Some of the acts prohibited are "truancy from school," "curfew violations," "running away from home," "incorrigibility at home," "association with undesirables," "idling away time," "unruliness," "immorality," and being "beyond parental control." Status offenses account for 30 to 40 percent of all juvenile court adjudications. In most of these cases the parent is the complaining party; it has been reported that 59 percent of New York City's juvenile cases result from parental complaints to authorities (Gough and Grilli 1973).

In summary, legal recognition of parental authority and family autonomy means (a) a hands-off approach when minors seek judicial interference in parental decisions and in parental conflicts over decisions involving their children, and (b) state support for parents' disciplinary efforts.

The doctrine of "parental prerogative" has also given rise to a considerable body of decisional law by the Supreme Court which requires the state to show adequate grounds for interference in the parent-child relationship. The U.S. Constitution offers no specific protection for parents against interference from the state in rearing their children, but parental rights have been given constitutional protection in a number of decisions. In *Meyer vs. Nebraska,* the Supreme Court ruled that a statute forbidding the teaching of German in school was an infringement on the parents' right to have German taught to their children, should they so desire. The decision was based on the liberty clause of the Fifth and Fourteenth Amendments which the Court held protects the "right to marry, establish a home, and direct the upbringing and education of children under [one's] control."

Relying on *Meyer,* the Court in *Pierce vs. Society of Sisters* struck down an Oregon statute requiring children to attend public schools. It stated that the requirement unduly interfered with the rights of parents to select private or parochial schools for their children and lacked a reasonable relation to any purpose within the competency of the state. It also noted:

The fundamental theory of liberty upon which all governments in this Union repose excludes any general power of the State to standardize its children. . . . The child is not the mere creature of the state; those who nurture him and direct his destiny have the right, coupled with the high duty, to recognize and prepare him for additional obligations.

Indeed, the Supreme Court has frequently emphasized the importance of the parents' right to the companionship, care, custody, and management of their children. This right has been deemed "essential," and recognized as one of the "basic civil rights of man," (*Skinner vs. Oklahoma,* 1942), "far more precious . . . than property rights" (*May vs. Anderson,* 1953). The Court's attitude is succinctly stated in *Prince vs. Massachusetts:*

It is cardinal with us that the custody, care and nurture of the child reside first in the parents, whose primary function and freedom include preparation for obligations the state can neither supply nor hinder.

The Court's view of the importance of the family relationship is reiterated in *Roe vs. Wade,* where it is also suggested that this relationship is protected by a constitutional right of privacy, which includes those rights implicit in the concept of an ordered liberty, "such as activities relating to marriage . . . procreation . . . contraception . . . family relationships . . . and child rearing and education."

The legal importance of parental rights is also demonstrated in the issue of court-appointed counsel. The Court has tended to be conservative in recognizing a constitutional right to such counsel except in cases where the litigant may lose his physical liberty, but has left open the possibility that due process may require the state to provide court-appointed counsel for an indigent parent before parental rights can be terminated. Although the Court did not affirm an absolute right to appointed counsel in *Lassiter vs. Department of Social Services,* it did hold that, when parental termination is threatened, the question of court-appointed counsel must be decided on a case-by-case basis. In doing so, the Court reaffirmed a long-standing precedent supporting the parent's liberty interest and his entitlement to due process protection. The Court stopped short of saying that counsel must be appointed in every termination case, but it endorsed a number of prestigious reports that urge appointment of such counsel to protect the parent-child relationship from state interference.

Even when the state intervenes in the parent-child relationship, the child's powerless, dependent, incompetent status is not altered. In such cases (dependency, neglect, abuse), the state acts in its role as *parens patriae*, and thus assumes parental authority in the place of the parent. Although the state purports to speak on the child's behalf in such cases, it speaks as though it were parent, to assert the child's best interest. The child is not considered capable of representing himself in such a contest.

INTRAFAMILY TORT IMMUNITY

In the area of the law that addresses conflicts arising out of physical injury done by one person to another—tort law—one also finds deference to parental prerogative and family autonomy, expressed in the "doctrine of intrafamily tort immunity." This doctrine precludes tort actions between a parent and a minor, unemancipated child. It originated in American jurisprudence with *Hewelette vs. George,* a case decided in Mississippi in 1891. *Hewelette* was an action brought by an unemancipated, minor girl against her mother for "false imprisonment by malicious confinement in an insane asylum for ten days." In refusing to allow the minor to sue her mother, the court stated:

So long as a parent is under obligation to care for, guide, and control and the child is under reciprocal obligation to aid and comfort and obey, no such action as this can be maintained. The peace of a sound public policy, designed to subserve the repose of families and the best interests of society, forbids to the minor child a right to appear in court in the injuries suffered at the hands of a parent. The State, through its Criminal laws, will give the minor child protection from parental violence and wrongdoing and this is all the child can be heard to demand.

Over the years, courts have attempted to justify the immunity doctrine, without notable success. The argument that the doctrine "promotes domestic tranquility" is weak: situations giving rise to a child's desire to sue his parent can hardly be thought of as tranquil. Another argument turns on the "family exchequer" theory: if one child is permitted to recover in a tort suit, family wealth will be reduced, and the other children in the family thus deprived of their fair share. This argument ignores the facts that most tort settlements are paid by insurance and that, in every state except Louisiana, children have no legal right to "share" in the family's resources. A parent can disinherit his children, or remember them in grossly disproportionate shares in his will. The argument that intrafamily tort actions cannot be entertained because of the danger of "fraud and collusion" in cases involving insurance claims does not hold up well either, and has been discredited in other areas of the law. The most frequently cited justification for the doctrine is the courts' "fear of eroding parental control of children" (McCurdy 1930).

Many credit the development of the intrafamily tort immunity doctrine to the similar doctrine of *interspousal* tort immunity, but the two are historically unrelated. Interspousal tort immunity developed in English law; parent-child tort immunity is exclusively a part of American law. (Many states have abolished interspousal tort immunity altogether.)

In spite of the obvious infirmities of arguments for parent-child tort immunity, however, more than two-thirds of the states still recognize it in some form. Some courts have relaxed the parent-child immunity doctrine in cases where the parent's injury to the child can be shown to have been intentional (HLJ 1967). A few courts have allowed children to receive damages against parents when the act involved was not peculiar to the parent-child relationship, such as cases where a child is injured in an automobile accident as a result of the parent's negligence. But when the injury arises directly out of the parent-child relationship, courts have been extremely reluctant to respond to a child's suit for damages.

"Negligent supervision" cases in which children, injured because of the parent's failure to supervise them properly, sue for damages suffered, exemplify this attitude. And it is in the context of these cases that courts have come closest to articulating a plausible and persuasive rationale for the parent-child immunity doctrine. The 1974 New York case of *Holodook vs. Spencer* is a good example. *Holodook* involved two separate instances of direct action by a child against his parent on grounds of "negligent supervision." In the first, a four-year-old boy was injured when he fell from the steps of an 11-foot-high slide. He sued his father, through a guardian *ad litem,* alleging that his father negligently allowed him to engage in dangerous play. In the second action, a three-year-old child was injured when playing in his backyard when hit by a riding mower operated by a neighbor's eight-year-old son. The injured child sued his mother, through his father as guardian *ad litem,* for negligent supervision. (The mothers of both children were inside the house when the accident occurred.)

In *Holodook* the New York Court of Appeals held that a child does not have a legally recognizable claim for damages against his parent for "negligent supervision," reasoning as follows:

> [We] can conceive of few, if any, accidental injuries to children which could not have been prevented, or substantially mitigated, by keener parental guidance, broader foresight, closer protection and better example. Indeed, a child could probably avoid most physical harm were he under his parent's constant surveillance and instruction, though detriment more subtle and perhaps more harmful than physical injury might result. If the instant negligent supervision were allowed, it would be the rare parent who could not conceivably be called to account in the courts for his conduct toward his child. . . .
>
> There is force to the argument that courts and juries should decide whether a particular defendant acted as a reasonable parent would have, under the circumstances. . . . In most areas of tort law, the reasonable man standard well serves the law's general principle of structuring human activity in accordance with the community's standards and expectations of proper conduct. In the family relation between parent and child, however, we do not believe that application of this standardized norm is the wisest course. The result, we believe, would be to circumscribe the wide range of discretion a parent ought to have in permitting his child to undertake responsibility and gain independence. . . . The duty to supervise a child in his daily activities has as its objective the fostering of physical, emotional and intellectual development, and is one whose enforcement can depend only on love. Each child is different, as is each parent: as to the former, some are to be pampered while some thrive on independence; as to the latter, some trust in their children to use care, others are very cautious. Considering the different economic, educational, cultural, ethnic and religious backgrounds which must prevail, there are so many combinations and permutations of parent-child relationship that may result that the search for a standard would necessarily be in vain. . . .
>
> The mutual obligations of the parent-child relation derive their strength and vitality from such forces as natural instinct, love and morality, and not from the essentially negative compulsions of the laws' directives and sanctions. Courts and Legislatures have recognized this, and consequently have intruded only minimally upon the family relation.

PARENTS' DUTIES TOWARD CHILDREN

The legal *quid pro quo* for parental prerogative is parental responsibility. The law imposes certain duties on parents, and it is considered to be "in return" for performing these duties that the parent receives the fullest possible state support for parental authority. The duties imposed on parents are demanding, and are central to the legal view of the parent-child relationship.

THE DUTY TO SUPPORT

The statutory law of every state requires that parents support their children. The duty to support requires the parent to furnish, in accordance with his or her means, adequate food, clothing, shelter, medical attention, and education, until the child attains majority.

The support duty can be enforced in several ways. Some statutes permit the child, through a guardian, to seek support as a civil remedy. The amount of support so ordered can be collected by ordinary creditors' remedies, e.g., levy and execution, and garnishment. Third parties who supply a child with so-called "necessaries" (medicine, food, clothing) are also given a cause of action against a defaulting parent to be reimbursed under the common-law "doctrine of necessaries." Finally, all states have criminal non-support statutes which permit imprisonment of a parent for failure to support his children.

THE DUTY TO PROVIDE CARE AND GUIDANCE

Parents are obligated to provide "proper guidance and guardianship" of their children, and legal sanctions can be enforced if a parent fails to meet certain minimum standards of care. Thus, as will be seen later, a parent who neglects or abuses his child may have his custody legally terminated in favor of some other adult. Also, criminal sanctions are imposed against parents who abuse their children, or influence them in a corrupt way. Otherwise, the duties imposed by the law in this area are minimal, and only in extreme cases are sanctions exercised.

THE DUTY TO SUPERVISE

Although minors are generally not allowed to sue their parents for negligent supervision, parents are held liable if injury to third parties results from their failure to properly supervise a child. For example, if a parent negligently entrusts his child with a "dangerous instrument," he may be held liable for any injury to a third party resulting from the child's wielding of the instrument.

CHILDREN'S DUTIES TOWARD PARENTS

THE DUTY OF OBEDIENCE

In return for support, a child is supposed to obey his parent. This duty is enforced through the court's refusal to hear cases in which the child attempts to overturn a parental decision, and through the court's willingness to support the parent's disciplinary efforts.

THE DUTY TO ASSIGN WAGES

A child is required, during minority, to turn over his earnings to his parents. This comes as a surprise to today's parents, but the rule dates from a time when children were considered an important economic asset to the family. In the American colonial period, parents were permitted to exploit their child for economic gain by "assigning" their rights to the child's services to another family or enterprise (Stern 1975). The child was accountable to his parents for all wages earned, and if the employer paid the minor instead of the father, the employer was held liable for those wages if sued by the father (*Watson vs. Kemp* 1899).

The Industrial Revolution created a situation in which the previously "socially neutral" practice of assigning a child's services came to be seen as a social evil. Children were no longer sent to live on farms or with other families, but were "sold" to factories, where they lived in boarding houses and dormitories and often worked under the most inhumane conditions. Their wages from factory work were significantly higher than their wages for farm and household work, and these wages were owed to the parents. Children thus became economic assets of the family unit in a new and valuable way, and abuse of the situation became increasingly common. Child labor laws have eliminated this abuse, and as a result the child's common-law obligation to turn over wages to his parents has lost its meaning.

EMANCIPATION

The doctrine of emancipation developed in response to the exploitation of children through early child labor practices. If emancipated, the child could retain the wages he would otherwise have had to give to his parents. In "total emancipation," the parent's duty of support and the child's duty of obedience were also terminated.

In theory, a minor could be emancipated only with his parents' consent. In reality, parental consent was sometimes found to be implied by ambiguous conduct. The procedural context in which the case arose influenced the court's finding in an emancipation matter. If creditors were seeking to attach a child's wages for his father's debts, courts were inclined to find that the child had been emancipated, and was therefore entitled to keep his own wages. But courts were not sympathetic toward parents seeking to avoid support duties on the grounds of emancipation. They were reluctant to declare that the child was emancipated if he would thereby be left dependent and without support. Most emancipation cases were disputes between parents and creditors or employers over ownership of a child's wages; very few reflected disputes between parents and children.

The doctrine of emancipation has been characterized as a "peculiar . . . unimportant corner of the law," and there are only a few such cases on the books (Katz et al. 1973). Application of the doctrine peaked in the era of child labor, when children's wages supplied the food for controversy and creditor's claims. Inevitably, as time progressed, the inhumane conditions under which so many children lived and worked caused a public outcry. Laws severely restricting child labor were closely followed by compulsory education laws, and children were moved from factories to schools. Compulsory education isolated children from adult activities and tended to delay "maturity;" thus emancipation ceased, for a time, to be an issue in the courts.

DAMAGES FOR THE DEATH OF A CHILD

One legal indicator of the social attitude toward a relationship is the measure of damages allowed for loss of, or injury to, the relationship. "Wrongful death" actions have a peculiar history in our legal system, and that history is essential to an understanding of the courts' behavior in this area.

Under the English common law, a person who was injured could recover damages from the person who had injured him (the tortfeasor). If, however, the tortfeasor were fortunate enough to bring about the death of the victim, the courts held that (i) a tort had been committed, but (ii) the tort died with the victim. No cause of action survived the deceased in favor of his estate. The "logic" of this rule meant that the surviving members of the victim's family, if left without support, had no legal remedy. As Lord Ellenborough declared in an 1808 English case, *Baker vs. Bolton,* "In a civil court the death of a human being can not be complained of as an injury."

The obvious result of this rule, as Prosser (1971) notes, was to make it "more profitable to kill the plaintiff than to scratch him," clearly an intolerable situation. The English finally responded by passing the Fatal Accidents Act of 1846; American jurisdictions followed suit with the "wrongful death acts."

The purpose of wrongful death acts is to enable family members who might have expected to receive support or assistance from the deceased to be compensated for his death. Damages are limited to the economic benefit the survivors might reasonably have expected to receive from the deceased during the remainder of his expected lifetime. In general, only pecuniary losses are considered. The difficulties inherent in evaluating impalpable injuries to "sentiment and affection" caused by the death have led courts to interpret the statutes narrowly; damages for grief and mental suffering are rarely allowed.

In cases involving the death of a spouse or parent, the wrongful death remedy can provide substantial relief. Awarding damages based on calculations of life expectancy and earning capacity seems reasonable and just. In the case of a child's death, however, the damages calculated by this "pecuniary loss" formula are not so sensible. Here, the formula requires that the cost of raising the child be deducted from the child's expected earnings during minority. The exercise is meaningless in most cases; the modern child, unlike his counterpart of the 1800s, is not typically an income-producing member of the family unit. As Prosser rightly points out: "[a]s any parent is well aware, any realistic view of the prospects must mean that the cost of rearing the child will far exceed any conceivable pecuniary benefits that might ever be optimistically expected of him; and damages honestly calculated could never be anything but a minus quantity" (1971:908–9). Another author has suggested that "strict adherence to the [pecuniary loss] rule could lead, *reductio ad absurdum*, to the conclusion that the tortfeasor should be reimbursed for having saved the parent money."

In 1960, the Michigan Supreme Court repudiated the pecuniary loss formula, pronouncing it "barbarous," and formulated a new basis for recovery in wrongful death actions involving minor children. The history of wrongful death actions tracks society's view of the parent-child relationship and is set out in the *Wycko* opinion at length:

The interpretation of the requirement of pecuniary loss found in the early cases . . . reflected the moral and legal standards of their times. In *Bramall v. Lees,* the court considered the case of a 12 year old girl, negligently killed. Despite the fact she had attained such age she remained, nevertheless, "living at home" and hence was "peculiarly then a burden to her parents." The father, however, succeeded in securing a verdict for 15 pounds. His theory was that in the course of a year or two, the child would have gone into a factory "and taken back money as its earnings for the parents." More fortunate was the father in *Duckworth v. Johnson.* Here a verdict for 20 pounds was obtained "by reason of the son, a boy fourteen years of age, having been killed by the falling of a wall in consequence of the defendant's negligence." The father, unlike Mr. Bramall, was able to show that his son had been working for two years and a half.
. . .

. . . [The judges in these cases] were merely interpreting the statutes in accordance with the social conditions of the day. . . . The rulings reflect the philosophy of the times, its ideals, and its social conditions. It was an era when ample work could be found for the agile bodies and nimble fingers of small children. . . . The apprenticeship of children to factory owners amounted to what Professor Trevelyan, Master of Trinity College, Cambridge, has described as "a slave traffic." "The atrocities visited upon these boys and girls," it is reported in the Encyclopedia of the Social Sciences, "literally driven to death in the mills, form one of the darkest chapters in the history of childhood." Age limits were set in an effort to control the traffic. In 1816 the apprenticeship of parish children under the age of nine was forbidden, but the underground employment of children under ten was not forbidden until 1843. . . . It is only against this somber background that we can fully understand the significance of the comment made in the Bramall Case that the girl was "living at home and getting nothing." At the age of twelve she was already long overdue at the mill.

This, then, was the day from which our precedents came, a day when the employment of children of tender years was the accepted practice and their pecuniary contributions to the family both substantial and provable. It is not surprising that the courts of such a society should have read into the statutory words "such damages as they [the jury] may think proportional to the injury resulting from such death" not only the requirement of a pecuniary loss, but, moreover, a pecuniary loss established by a wage-benefit-less-costs measure of damages. Other losses were unreal and intangible and at this time in our legal history the courts would have no truck with what Chief Baron Pollock termed in Duckworth "imaginary losses."

That this barbarous concept of the pecuniary loss of a parent from the death of his child should control our decisions today is a reproach to justice. . . . A combination of influences, all arising from the public condemnation of child labor, has resulted in almost universal state child-labor and compulsory school attendance laws. In fact, our society, by one means or another, now attempts to keep children out of the general labor market. Yet there still exists in the law this remote and repulsive backwash of time and civilization, untouched by the onward march of society. . . .

It follows from the foregoing that we now reject . . . the child-labor measure of the pecuniary loss suffered through the death of the minor child, namely, his probable wages less the cost of his upkeep.

The *Wycko* court then enunciated a new formula which, in its perception, more closely reflected the modern parent-child relationship:

The pecuniary value of a human life is a compound of many elements. . . . Just as with respect to a manufacturing plant, or industrial machine, value involves the cost of acquisition, replacement, upkeep, maintenance service, repair and renovation, so, in our context, we must consider the expenses of birth, of food, of clothing, of medicines, of instruction, of nurture and shelter. Moreover, just as an item of machinery forming part of a functioning industrial plant has a value over and above that of a similar item in a showroom, awaiting purchase, so an individual member of a family has a value to others as part of a functioning social and economic unit. This value is the value of mutual society and protection, in a word, companionship. The human companionship thus afforded has a definite, substantial and ascertainable pecuniary value and its loss forms a part of the "value" of the life we seek to ascertain. We are, it will be noted, restricting the losses to pecuniary losses, the actual money value of the life of the child, not the sorrow and anguish caused by its death. Food, shelter, clothing, and companionship, however, are obtainable on the open market, have an ascertainable money value. . . . It is true, of course, that there will be uncertainties in all of these proofs, due to the nature of the case, but we are constrained to observe that it is not the privilege of him whose wrongful act caused the loss to hide behind the uncertainties inherent in the very situation his wrong has created.

The *Wycko* case has been interpreted as creating a new theory of recovery in infant wrongful death cases, the theory of the "lost investment." Under this theory, the parent is permitted to recover for the monetary investment he has made in the child—expenses of birth, food, clothing, medicine, instruction, nurture, and shelter. The emphasis on "investment" is preferable to the lost-earnings approach of child labor days. The theory offers no new view of the parent-child relationship, but it departs from the view that children are merely the property of their parents.

TERMINATION OF THE PARENT-CHILD RELATIONSHIP

There is ample evidence, as presented above, that the American legal system is oriented toward protecting parental prerogatives and family autonomy. It should be noted that this approach has not been taken in the absence of alternatives, but is rather a fundamental and consistently reaffirmed choice.

It would be entirely possible for the state to assume many, if not most, child-rearing responsibilities. Plato and other social theorists have advocated this approach, and it has been applied in a few modern contexts such as the Israeli kibbutzim and some collectives in the Soviet Union. A more communal approach to child-rearing is also found in many preliterate societies. And most Western industrial societies, while placing primary responsibility for the care and nurture of children on the parents, provide greater publicly supported child care and other support services than are available in the United States.

A modern proposal, the "trusteeship" approach, would be another departure from our accepted practice. Its advocates, who define parents as "trustees" of their children rather than as having "rights" to their children, propose that the law require parents to demonstrate that they are good parents before they are accorded "parental prerogatives." Parents would be held responsible for providing more than minimal care (food, clothing, shelter), and would be expected to provide an environment of love and adequate stimulation in which the child could develop to his maximum potential. Implementation of such a system might involve screening children for developmental progress, offering services to cope with problems discovered in screening, and the use of coercive intervention if parents refused to cooperate.

It is not possible to evaluate the desirability of these alternatives in this writing, but it is important to understand that our society's emphasis on parental prerogatives need not be taken for granted. It can be viewed as a distinct choice among alternatives. Even though many people claim that the American system of parental autonomy has broken down and that no one performs many traditional family functions, our legal system remains firmly committed to the concept of parental autonomy. This fact is attested to by the numerous federal and state programs aimed specifically at "strengthening the family" in order to enable it to perform its child-rearing and socializing functions more effectively.

Parental autonomy is supported, as discussed earlier, by giving parents the broadest possible freedoms with regard to child rearing, and by supporting their disciplinary efforts when necessary. Intervention is seen to be justified in only the most extreme cases. Intervention is permissible only if the parents fail to meet certain minimal standards, and not, as in the trusteeship example, if they fail to live up to an ideal of parenting.

The circumstances under which the parent may be said to have failed to meet required minimal standards are delineated in the statutes defining the "dependence, neglect, and abuse" of children. A "dependent child" is defined as one in need of "placement, special care or treatment" because he has no parent or guardian, or because his parent or guardian is unable to provide for his supervision and care. A "neglected child" is a child who does not receive proper care or supervision, who has been abandoned, who lives in an environment "injurious to his welfare," or who has been placed for care of adoption in violation of law. An "abused child" has been subjected to physical assault or some form of sexual assault. The language of these definitions is vague, suggesting that a virtually unlimited intervention would be possible, and some experts have argued for more precisely phrased statutes in order to protect parents against state intervention (Goldstein, Freud, and Solnit 1979).

Although the breadth of the statutes on child abuse and neglect seem to permit states to intervene extensively in the parent-child relationship, a strong principle of deference to parental authority prevents such intervention. ("Overintervention" does occur, but generally in circumstances in which the home environment departs from traditional middle-class norms.) It is important to note that the traditional recognition of a parent's right to administer reasonable corporal punishment also limits state intervention. To warrant intervention, physical abuse must involve a nonaccidental injury which causes or creates a substantial risk of death, disfigurement, or impairment of bodily functioning. As a result, the threshold for state intervention is very high.

In principle and practice, then, our system allows for maximum parental discretion. It does not seek to define or uphold any ideal of child rearing or parenting. Today, as in the past, the practice of providing parents with a maximum of power over their children, while providing the children with a minimum of protection against the abuse of that power, is still seen as consistent with the best interests of our society. The child is protected by law only from the most extreme and dangerous types of mistreatment.

2

The Legal View of Minors

THE legal view of minors is a carryover from the general view that children are helpless and are totally dependent on their parents. Legally, minors' social interactions and responsibilities are regulated by restrictions of their freedom, capacity and competency limitations, rules of social accountability, and judicial rulings on minors' civil rights.

RESTRICTIONS ON MINORS' FREEDOM

Minors are subject to numerous restrictions of their freedom to function, restrictions that disappear when they attain the magical "age of majority." With a few exceptions, these restrictions are meant to protect minors from their own improvidence or from the corrupting influence of others. The exceptions are restrictions designed to protect society from a minor's improvidence.

These restrictions vary greatly in their impact on a minor's ability to function productively in society, in their influence on the shaping of his or her attitudes, and in the degree to which they define, if only indirectly, certain social ideals of child rearing. For example, minors are restricted from voting, holding public office, obtaining drivers' licenses without meeting special requirements, working, purchasing cigarettes and alcoholic beverages, entering barrooms and billiard halls, being tattooed, and purchasing or viewing certain sexually explicit materials.

Restrictions on obtaining a driver's license take on an added dimension in an automobile-centered society over and above the general stigma of being under age. The automobile is almost essential in American life. Qualifying for a driver's license is an event that ranks with the onset of puberty in the lives of most young Americans. Flatly to prohibit persons under 18 years of age from driving would be problematic, given the importance of driving in today's society, yet a disproportionate number of automobile accidents are caused by young drivers. How much "protection" is enough?

The right to vote, while not nearly so treasured a privilege among our youth as the right to drive, is nevertheless the most important political power of the citizenry. It has been crucial to every political and ethnic group that has sought to advance in our society and political structure. The voting age can be set no higher than 18 under the Constitution, but only a few states allow persons under 18 to vote. Legislatures seem to agree that persons under 18 lack the judgment necessary to be responsible voters. Attaining the capacity to vote thus becomes synonymous with attaining "adult" status, and the right to participate fully in the conduct of the society.

Restrictions on minors' right to work have been the center of a great deal of controversy in recent years. The social climate that invited the abuse of child labor is, to all appearances, a thing of the past. Current laws, ostensibly designed to protect children, often have the effect of excluding young people from the work force in such a way as to prolong childhood dependency unnecessarily, and thereby contribute to the increasingly serious problem of youth unemployment and "idleness." The desirability of our tendency to prolong childhood dependency has been seriously challenged by both economists and social scientists:

Increased economic efficiency and freedom for children have not been achieved without cost. What children have lost in the process is the chance to be economically useful. And through a prolonged period of nearly complete economic dependency, they may grow to doubt their own worth. Furthermore, as parents no longer have as direct an economic stake in their children, they no longer have as strong an incentive to insure that their children learn some kind of useful work. Witness the frustration of graduates from high school, and even college, who cannot find jobs, which suggests that many children may be growing to adulthood without learning any practical skills. This does more than indicate the possible need for teaching practical skills in school—rather it calls into question the whole idea of childhood as a period of involuntary dependency. (Stern et al. 1975).

An even more interesting, though probably less important, controversy over minors' rights is the question of restricting a minor's access to sexually explicit material that is available to adults. In its ruling in *Ginsberg vs. New York,* the Supreme Court of the United States held that it was constitutional for the state of New York to restrict the right of minors under 17 years of age to determine for themselves what sexually explicit material they could see or read. In its opinion, the Court struggled with only limited success to explain precisely why First Amendment rights, the most treasured of our civil rights, could be restricted in the case of minors. Its rationale boils down to little more than a statement that "children are children." The Court resorted to what it considered a consensus among experts, and cited an article by Emerson in the *Yale Law Review,* "Toward a General Theory of the First Amendment:"

[M]any commentators, including many committed to the proposition that "[n]o general restriction or expression in terms of 'obscenity' can . . . be reconciled with the first amendment," recognize that "the power of the state to control the conduct of children reaches beyond the scope of its authority over adults," and accordingly acknowledge a supervening state interest in the regulation of literature sold to children.

According to Emerson,

[D]ifferent factors come into play, also, where the interest at stake is the effect of erotic expression on children. The world of children is not strictly a part of the adult realm of free expression. The factor of immaturity, and perhaps other considerations, impose different rules . . . it suffices to say that regulations of communication addressed to them need not conform to the requirements of the first amendment in the same way as those applicable to adults.

The Court then fell back on the traditional legal interpretation of the parent-child relationship to justify its ruling:

The well-being of its children is not of course a subject within the State's constitutional power to regulate, and, in our view, two interests justify limitations upon the availability of sex material to minors under 17. . . . First of all, constitutional interpretation has consistently recognized that the parents' claim to authority in their own household to direct the rearing of their children is basic in the structure of our society. . . . The legislature could properly conclude that parents and others, teachers for example, who have . . . primary responsibility for children's well-being are entitled to the support of laws designed to aid discharge of that responsibility.

In the Court's opinion, no first amendment violation of the rights of children is present in limiting their access to pornographic materials if the rights of access of parents are not limited in the process:

Moreover, the prohibition against sales to minors does not bar parents who so desire from purchasing the magazines for their children.

The opinion goes on to declare that the "state also has an independent interest in the well-being of its youth," and an interest "to protect the welfare of children," and to see that they are "safeguarded from abuses which might prevent their growth into free and independent well-developed men and citizens." The Court did not demand any proof from the state that obscenity is demonstrably harmful to minors:

. . . To be sure, there is no lack of "studies" which purport to demonstrate that obscenity is or is not "a basic factor in impairing the ethical and moral development of . . . youth and a clear and present danger to the people of the state." But the growing consensus of commentators is that "while these studies all agree that a causal link has not been demonstrated, they are equally agreed that a causal link has not been disproved either." We do not demand of legislatures "scientifically certain criteria". . . . We therefore cannot say that . . . [defining] obscenity on the basis of its appeal to minors under 17 has no rational relation to the objective of safeguarding such minors from harm.

It is perhaps unjust to accuse the Court of failing to articulate the reasons for distinguishing between the constitutional rights of children and of adults in this way. Mr. Justice Stewart, in his concurring opinion, was probably expressing the feelings of the Court when he said:

I think a State may permissibly determine that, at least in some precisely delineated areas, a child . . . is not possessed of that full capacity for

individual choice which is the presupposition of First Amendment guarantees. It is only upon such a premise, I should suppose, that a State may
deprive children of other rights—the right to marry, for example, or the
right to vote—deprivations that would be constitutionally intolerable for
adults.

In any event, those commentators who argue that obscenity legislation is not constitutional because it "imposes a single standard
of public morality" are willing to acknowledge the relevance of the
parental role and to accept laws regulating obscenity which relate
only to minors:

One must consider how much difference it makes if laws are designed to
protect only the morals of a child. While many of the constitutional arguments against morals legislation apply equally to legislation protecting the
morals of children, one can well distinguish laws which do not impose a
morality on children, but which support the right of parents to deal with
the morals of their children as they see fit. (Emerson 1963)

CAPACITY AND COMPETENCY LIMITATIONS

The three major "limitations of capacity" imposed on a minor are
his incapacity to contract, his incapacity to marry, and his incapacity to consent to certain acts requiring consent, primarily medical
and surgical procedures. Children are also deemed incapable of
consenting to sexual relations if they are below a specified age (the
age varies from state to state). Capacity and competency limitations often have the same effect as outright restrictions, but there
are important differences between a limitation and a restriction. In
a matter of capacity limitation, the minor may do the deed with
impunity if he is physically capable of doing it—i.e., there is no
one charged with the duty to prevent him, and no legal principles
which hold adults accountable for allowing or helping him. The
law is basically uninterested in a minor's conduct in these matters
unless he himself seeks to undo the deed. In the case of a restriction, society punishes the minor and/or the participating adult, and
uses a variety of "gatekeepers" (voting registrars, bartenders, thea-
ter operators) to see that the minor is thwarted if he attempts to
violate the prohibition.

A minor's contracts are not enforceable against him; no party with whom he contracts can force him or obtain judicial support to force him to perform, or collect damages from him for nonperformance (Restatement of Contracts). If the minor does perform, in whole or in part, he is nevertheless entitled to the return of any property or money he has given under contract (*Keser vs. Chagnon* 1966). On the other hand, the party contracting with the minor cannot avoid performing his part of the bargain if the minor chooses to enforce the contract.

This rule is obviously designed to protect the minor from his own inexperience and lack of judgment, but it also has the effect of completely undermining any attempt by the minor at commercial dealings. Contracts are the basis of most business transactions, and very few people are willing to contract with someone who can avoid his obligations so easily while they themselves remain liable.

Moreover, the person contracting with a minor has no recourse against the parent, who is not responsible for his child's attempts to contract unless he himself knowingly and voluntarily accepts that responsibility. And the parent cannot "consent for his child" to bind the child to a contractual commitment.

Marriage is a form of contract, and a minor is assumed to lack the capacity to consent to marriage. The limitations on marriage include an element of restriction; state laws usually restrict or prohibit the issuing of marriage licenses to minors, and sometimes impose small penalties on persons officiating at an underage marriage. Under the common law, a minor was deemed capable of marriage at the age of 12, as that age was associated with the onset of puberty. Today, capacity to marry is governed by statute in all states, most of which set the age at 18. A minor who marries below the established age has the right to annul the marriage, but most states recognize the marriage as valid until such annulment is obtained. (Only a few states refuse altogether to recognize an underage marriage.)

The rationale behind the capacity limitation on marriage is not based on a desire to protect society from the often harmful consequences of early marriage, though there is ample evidence to support such a rationale. (The divorce rate and the incidence of unwanted births are at their highest among teenagers.) The justification for the marriage limitation is no more and no less than that for the contract limitation—to protect minors from their own improvidence and ignorance.

A minor is also deemed incapable of giving effective consent in all other cases where informed consent is necessary. A most important application of this is in the area of "intentional interference with the minor's person or property" covered by the law of torts. The fundamental principle of the common law, *volenti non fit injuria* ("to one who is willing, no wrong is done"), does not apply (Prosser 1971). Normally, if a person willingly engages in a boxing match, he may not later complain that he was assaulted; consent is a valid defense against such a complaint. Since a minor is assumed under the law to be incapable of giving consent, this defense is not allowed. An exception is made for an activity requiring consent which is for the minor's benefit; in this case, parental approval operates as an effective consent. A doctor who treats or performs surgery on a minor may not be found liable for the intentional tort of assault if the consent of the minor's parents has been obtained (MLR 1977; Skegg 1973). (An exception is made for emergency cases in which there is not time to obtain the parent's consent; the courts hold that consent is implied, on the theory that the parent would have consented had he known the child's life was at stake.)

SOCIAL ACCOUNTABILITY

Although as a general rule minors are presumed incompetent and thus not legally responsible, this principle does not relieve minors entirely of social accountability. Whereas a minor enjoys a complete lack of accountability in the areas of contract and marriage, he is not always shielded from the consequences of his actions where criminal and tort law apply. This is because of the absence of voluntary participation by the "victim" of the minor's misdeeds in the criminal and tort law area.

CRIMINAL LAW

The minor's position with respect to the criminal law is particularly troublesome and controversial. Under the common law, a child under the age of 7 was deemed incapable of committing a crime;

for children between the ages of 7 and 14, there was a presumption of incapacity, but it could be rebutted if it were shown that the child knew the difference between good and evil; beyond the age of 14, the child was held fully responsible for his criminal acts unless a lack of capacity could be shown. Until the early nineteenth century, children deemed capable of committing crimes were tried, convicted, and sentenced in the same manner as adults. Since there were no special institutions for them, they were simply packed off to jail and left to mingle freely with the other prisoners.

This situation eventually provoked attempts at reform, and around the turn of the century a new theoretical basis for the treatment of juvenile offenders began to evolve. The emphasis shifted away from punishment and toward help and rehabilitation (*Kent vs. United States,* 1966). A separate juvenile court system was established which endorsed the belief that children, because of their age, are generally incapable of criminal behavior and are more amenable to treatment and rehabilitation than are adults. In the juvenile court system, the state assumes the role, as *parens patriae,* of helping the child (Midonick 1972).

In theory, the juvenile justice system is supposed to be judgment free, and the ideas of guilt, accountability, and social responsibility have been deliberately set aside (Shears 1920). In reality, however, the system does indeed impose a "punishment" on the minor for antisocial behavior. In the first place, the minor faces an adjudication of delinquency. Guilt is not mentioned, but the term "delinquency" is most often defined in terms of the criminal law. A delinquent child is typically defined as "any child who has committed any criminal offense under state law or under an ordinance of local government, including violations of the motor vehicle laws, or a child who has violated the conditions of probation."

Once an adjudication of delinquency is made, an appropriate disposition of the child must be made. Sometimes he is returned to his home, but often he is confined to a state institution where his freedom is severely restricted. The following description from *In re Gault* illustrates well the effect of this disposition:

A boy is charged with misconduct. The boy is committed to an institution where he may be restrained of liberty for years. It is of no constitutional consequence—and of limited practical meaning—that the institution to which he is committed is called an Industrial School. The fact of the matter is that, however euphemistic the title, a "receiving home" or an "industrial school" for juveniles is an institution of confinement in which the child is incarcerated for a greater or lesser time. His world becomes "a building with whitewashed walls, regimented routine and institutional hours. Instead of mother and father and sisters and brothers and friends and classmates, his world is peopled by guards, custodians, state employees," and delinquents confined with him.

Clearly, such treatment is a form of punishment. Theory aside, the juvenile offender is most certainly made to "pay the piper" for his misdeeds.

TORT LAW

A minor's position in the law of torts closely resembles his position in the criminal law. He may be held liable in compensatory damages for his intentional torts, because the tort law provides compensation for people who are injured by intentional or negligent actions of others, irrespective of whether their intention was wrongful. A minor who has committed an intentional tort, such as pushing another child off a ledge, is considered capable of having intended to push the child. Therefore, the law maintains that the loss resulting from the minor's tort should fall on the estate of the wrongdoer rather than on the estate of the guiltless and injured person. This approach is especially sensible and compelling in those cases where the minor is insured, or has property or money of his own. Thus, if a four-year-old commits an intentional tort such as battery, he may be held liable for compensatory damages. The same child, however, may be exempt from punitive damages, which are premised on malicious intent, if the child lacks the capacity to know that his conduct was wrong.

Negligent torts are evaluated in light of the minor's capacity to foresee the consequences of his conduct. If the court determines that a minor lacked mental capacity to realize that conduct not intended to be harmful might nevertheless be reasonably expected to cause harm, the minor will not be held liable for negligence (*Ellis vs. Dangelo* 1952). How the court should make such a determination is, however, the subject of some debate.

Some courts have relied on a presumption similar to that regarding criminal liability under the old common law. A minor under the age of 7 is conclusively presumed incapable of negligence; children from 7 through 14 are presumed incapable, but the presumption is rebuttable; and children over the age of 14 are presumed capable, but may rebut the presumption. The 7 to 14 presumption has been abandoned in most states during the last twenty years in favor of a rule which allows a 7- to 14-year-old to be held liable for negligence if his conduct "could be deemed violative of the degree of care usually exercised by ordinarily prudent children of the same age, intelligence, and experience under the same or similar circumstances." Juries are assigned the task of making these distinctions (*Williamson vs. Garland* 1966).

It probably goes without saying that parents may not be held criminally liable for their children's violations of the criminal law; nor are they vicariously liable for their children's injurious acts under the law of torts. (The exception under the tort law is, of course, a case in which the parent can be shown guilty of negligent supervision, and the injury is to a third party.)

In any event, tort suits against minors are rare, largely because minors usually lack the financial resources or insurance coverage that might make them attractive defendants. The issue of a minor's negligence is usually limited to cases involving his or her "contributory negligence," situations in which a minor has been injured by a third party and the question is whether his own conduct contributed to the injury.

MINORS' CIVIL RIGHTS

GENERAL

In spite of the extensive limitations and restrictions on minors' freedom of conduct in the world at large—the prohibitions on voting, working, marrying, drinking, and driving—the Supreme Court has seen fit to protect minors under the Bill of Rights. Generally, the Court has taken the view that the Bill of Rights should not be assumed to apply only to adults, unless the state has a good reason to deny these rights to minors. The denial to minors of two of our most important civil rights, the rights to vote and to marry, is not truly a contradiction of this stance. The denial of the right to vote is indirectly established by the Constitution itself in setting the voting age at 18. With respect to the right to marry, which the Court has often called "a basic civil right of man," no direct ruling on the constitutionality of limiting this right to persons who have attained the age of majority has ever been handed down. However, it is not likely that the Court would object to age limitations on marriage in light of the strong social justifications for upholding them. Society as a whole, as well as minors, may be presumed to benefit in most cases from postponing this important decision. Forbidding minors access to "obscene" literature has also been mentioned as an example of limiting their First Amendment rights.

In most other cases, however, the Court has had very little difficulty in finding that basic civil rights extend to minors as to other citizens. The Court has found nothing in the condition of minority itself that justifies withholding these rights.

Using this line of reasoning, the Court has not hesitated to protect the First Amendment religious rights of school children who refuse to salute the flag. In *West Virginia vs. Barnette,* the leading case on this problem, the Court was so undisturbed by the minority status of the plaintiffs that no mention is made of their minority in the opinion. Again, in *Tinker vs. Des Moines School District,* the Court upheld the speech rights of minors who sought to express their opposition to the Vietnam War by wearing black armbands to school. In this case, the Court was undisturbed by the minority status, even though the defendants' status as students raised the key issue in the case, i.e., the need for school discipline versus First Amendment rights. In the Court's view, this issue would presumably have been present had the students been 13 or 33.

The Supreme Court has not ruled on minors' Fourth Amendment search and seizure rights, but every court that has considered the question has held that the principles which protect adults apply to the same extent to minors.

Similarly, the due process protections of the Fifth and Fourteenth amendments also apply to minors. Minor defendants in juvenile proceedings are entitled to notice of the charges against them and the opportunity to be heard; they are entitled to confront and cross-examine the witnesses against them; and they are protected by the privilege against self-incrimination, and by the presumption of innocence until proven guilty.

With regard to each of the above-mentioned rights normally afforded criminal defendants, some have argued that the extension of these rights to minors could seriously undermine the rehabilitative ideal upon which the juvenile justice system is based. The Supreme Court has considered this argument in relation to each of the above-mentioned rights, and there has been only one case in which a procedural protection available in adult criminal proceedings has been expressly withheld from the juvenile process: In *McKeiver vs. Pennsylvania*, the Court held that the right to trial by a jury in a criminal case was not constitutionally required in juvenile proceedings. The rationale for the decision was not related to the defendant's minority status as such, but pertained to the nature of the juvenile proceedings. The Sixth Amendment guarantees the right to an impartial trial by jury in "all criminal proceedings," and juvenile proceedings are not held to be criminal proceedings. A juvenile proceeding is technically classified as a civil proceeding because its purpose is supposedly nonpunitive. The Court did not therefore feel constitutionally compelled to require a trial by jury, and feared that the injection of the jury trial requirement would transform the hearing into a fully adversary process, thus destroying the attempt to keep the proceedings informal, intimate, and protective.

The most recent case upholding the Fourteenth Amendment rights of minors is that of *Goss vs. Lopez*, involving due process requirements in school disciplinary proceedings. Here again, the Court ignored the plaintiff's minority status, and focused its opinion on the appropriateness of requiring some measure of procedural fairness in school disciplinary proceedings regardless of the age of the accused. The Court ruled that students facing temporary suspension have interests qualifying for protection under the Due Process Clause. The Court held that due process requires, for a suspension of ten days or less, at least that the student be given oral or written notice of the charges against him, an explanation of the evidence the authorities have, and an opportunity to present his side.

In light of its decisions in the civil rights area, the U.S. Supreme Court does not appear to view minors as second-class citizens. Minors come to the Court with the same presumption of constitutional protection enjoyed by adults.

PARENTAL INVOLVEMENT

Although the cases just discussed clearly indicate that the Supreme Court has shown no reservations when dealing generally with the question of civil rights for minors, it would be seriously misleading to view these as cases dealing with "children's rights." First of all, in most of the cases the Court barely took notice of the minority status of the defendants; that status was obviously not an issue. Second, and more important for the "children's rights" issue, in almost every case cited the parents were parties to the actions with their children, and the parents were asserting constitutional rights for themselves as well as for their children. In its opinions, the Court has tended to speak of the parents and children together as a unit, rather than to draw a distinction between the one and the other.

"The talk of the child in the street is that of his father and mother," says the Babylonian Talmud, and this truth is evident from the Supreme Court's civil rights cases affecting minors. For example, in *West Virginia vs. Barnette,* the "Jehovah's Witness flag salute case," the plaintiffs were the parents and their children, complaining of the penalties imposed on them for failure to salute the flag:

Children of this faith have been expelled from school and are threatened with exclusion for no other cause. Officials threaten to send them to reformatories maintained for criminally inclined juveniles. Parents of such children have been prosecuted and are threatened with prosecution for causing delinquency.

These children were obviously influenced by their parents' religious beliefs, and were carrying those beliefs into the schools. Parents and children were united in their complaint against the state.

The situation was similar in *Tinker vs. Des Moines School District,* the case of the war protestors who wished to wear black armbands to school. The petitioners were John Tinker, 15; Christopher

Tinker, 16; and Mary Beth Tinker, 13. The children's parents were activists working with the American Friends Service Committee and the Women's International League for Peace and Freedom. The family had engaged in previous activities protesting the war, and the parent-child collaboration in the armband incident was clear. When the children were suspended from school and ordered not to return wearing the armbands, their parents kept them out of school for the duration of the scheduled war protest. When the children filed their civil rights action in federal court, the suit was filed by their father as guardian *ad litem.* The children were clearly collaborating with their parents against the state.

In *Gault,* the seminal case in the area of juvenile due process, it was the parents of Gerald Gault who petitioned for a writ of habeas corpus to secure the release of the 15-year-old plaintiff from the state industrial school. They complained that they, as Gerald's parents, had been denied the fundamentals of due process even as had the boy. As the Court ruled on these issues, it extended the now celebrated "Gault rights" to both the juvenile and his parents. On the question of notice of charges, the Court said that *the child and his parents or guardian* must be notified, in writing, of the specific charge or factual allegation to be considered at the hearing.

Due process . . . does not allow a hearing to be held in which a youth's freedom and his parent's right to custody, are at stake without giving them timely notice, in advance of hearing, of the specific issues that they must meet.
[T]he Due Process Clause of the Fourteenth Amendment requires that in respect of proceedings to determine delinquency which may result in commitment to an institution in which the juvenile's freedom is curtailed, the child *and his parents* must be notified of the child's right to be represented by counsel *retained by them,* or if they are unable to afford counsel, that counsel will be appointed to represent the child. (Emphasis added)

Finally, although the privilege against self-incrimination and the right to cross-examination are not discussed in terms of the parent's rights and the child's rights in *Gault,* the parent is presumably entitled to object to the use of a confession illegally obtained, if that confession may lead to the removal of the child to a state institution; the same principle would hold true for the rights of confrontation and cross-examination.

The unavoidable involvement of the parent in a juvenile rights case is illuminated by Fourth Amendment search and seizure limitations. A person who consents to a search of his property may not later complain that the search was unreasonable, but consent to a search need not necessarily be given by the occupant of the property. A person who has a right to be present, or to control the property, may give such consent. The validity of searches conducted on the basis of the parents' consent to have the police search their child's room has been upheld by the courts in numerous cases, on the grounds of the parents' right to use the room or to control the premises being searched.

Also, the Fourth Amendment protects only against intrusions by the state, and not against unreasonable searches by private individuals. Evidence obtained by parents who search their children's possessions is not excludable on Fourth Amendment grounds. There are numerous cases in which children have been adjudicated juvenile offenders on the basis of evidence confiscated by their parents.

The *Ginsberg* case involving restrictions on a minor's access to sexually explicit material is a good illustration of the overriding influence of parental rights over the rights of children. In *Ginsberg*, the Court clearly endorsed the view that prohibiting the sale of pornographic material to minors is constitutional so long as the prohibition does not bar parents who so desire from purchasing the material for their child.

It is no accident that the parents' interests and those of the child were seen to coincide in the civil rights cases cited. Few would even have arisen if the children had not been repeating the "talk . . . of the father and the mother." Because of the identity of interest between parent and child, it is fair to suggest that these cases have little to contribute to the debate over "children's rights;" the central issue in that debate is whether children have autonomy from their parents. The Supreme Court's decisions in the areas of First, Fourth, and Fifth Amendment freedoms have little to say on that question. Moreover, in the one line of cases where conflicts between parents and children are presented indirectly—the search and seizure cases—the parents' authority with respect to the child and his belongings is clearly upheld.

One case decided by the Supreme Court in recent years in which a direct conflict is raised between parental prerogative and a minor's claim that his constitutional rights are violated by the exercise of such prerogative is *Parham vs. J. R. and J. L., Minors,* decided in 1979. *Parham* arose out of the mental health system of the state of Georgia and involved two unrelated teenage children, J. R. and J. L., each of whom had been institutionalized at the Georgia State Mental Hospital on the basis of "voluntary" admission papers signed by his parents or guardians. A lawsuit was brought on behalf of J. R. and J. L., challenging the procedure by which they were committed to the state hospital on the grounds that it violated their due process rights. Prior decisions of the Supreme Court had clearly established that an adult has the right to due process before he/she can be committed to a mental hospital. The Court reiterated criteria from those previous cases to reaffirm the principle and, in keeping with its prior decisions extending civil rights to children, said:

It is not disputed that a child, in common with adults, has a substantial liberty interest in not being confined unnecessarily for medical treatment and that the State's involvement in the commitment decision constitutes state action under the Fourteenth Amendment.

The Court went on, however, to say the following:

In applying these criteria, we must first consider the child's interest in not being committed. Normally, however, since this interest is inextricably linked with the parents' interest in and obligation for the welfare and health of the child, the private interest at stake is a combination of the child's and the parents' concerns.

In dealing with the interests of the parents, the Court said explicitly what had been implicit in so many of its prior opinions:

The law's concept of the family rests on a presumption that parents possess what a child lacks in maturity, experience, and capacity for judgment required for making life's difficult decisions. More important, historically it has recognized that natural bonds of affection lead parents to act in the best interests of their children.

As with so many other legal presumptions, experience and reality may rebut what the law accepts as a starting point; the incidence of child neglect and abuse cases attests to this. That some parents "may at times be acting against the interests of their child" creates a basis for caution, but is hardly a reason to discard wholesale those pages of human experience that teach that parents generally do act in the child's best interests. The statist notion that governmental power should supersede parental authority in *all* cases because *some* parents abuse and neglect children is repugnant to American tradition . . .

. . . Simply because the decision of a parent is not agreeable to a child or because it involves risks does not automatically transfer the power to make that decision from the parents to some agency or officer of the state. The same characterizations can be made for a tonsillectomy, appendectomy or other medical procedure. Most children, even in adolescence, simply are not able to make sound judgments concerning many decisions, including their need for medical care or treatment. Parents can and must make those decisions. . . . The fact that a child may balk at hospitalization or complain about a parental refusal to provide cosmetic surgery does not diminish the parents' authority to decide what is best for the child. . . . Neither state officials nor federal courts are equipped to review such parental decisions. . . .

In defining the respective rights and prerogatives of the child and parent in the voluntary commitment setting, we conclude that our precedents permit the parents to retain a substantial, if not the dominant, role in the decision, absent a finding of neglect or abuse, and that the traditional presumption that the parents act in the best interests of their child should apply.

The Court went on to hold that the child's constitutional rights to be protected against the risk of an erroneous commitment were adequately protected by existing statutory procedures conditioning even voluntary admission on the opinion of a physician. The Court ruled clearly against requiring a full-blown adversarial hearing in such cases:

[A] problem with requiring a formalized, factfinding hearing lies in the danger it poses for significant intrusion into the parent-child relationship. Pitting the parents and child as adversaries often will be at odds with the presumption that parents act in the best interests of their child. It is one thing to require a neutral physician to make a careful review of the parents' decision in order to make sure it is proper from a medical standpoint; it is a wholly different matter to employ an adversary contest to ascertain whether the parents' motivation is consistent with the child's interests.

Moreover, it is appropriate to inquire into how such a hearing would contribute to the long range successful treatment of the patient. Surely, there is a risk that it would exacerbate whatever tensions already existed between the child and the parents. Since the parents can and usually do play a significant role in the treatment while the child is hospitalized and even more so after release, there is a serious risk that an adversary confrontation will adversely affect the ability of the parents to assist the child while in the hospital. Moreover, it will make his subsequent return home more difficult. These unfortunate results are especially critical with an emotionally disturbed child; they seem likely to occur in the context of an adversary hearing in which the parents testify.

The line of cases from *Pierce* through *Parham* serves as a reminder of the social and psychological reality of the parent-child relationship, at least as it exists in our society. Whether the relationship is healthy or unhealthy, and whether parents exercise good or poor judgment, the fact remains that parents exercise tremendous influence over their children. The courts tend not only to recognize but to reinforce parental authority and, even in an area as precious as the Bill of Rights, to defer to parental authority when conflict is presented.

3

The Maturity Factor

HISTORICALLY, the law has established an age of discretion in a somewhat arbitrary manner because as Blackstone puts it, "some [point] must necessarily be established." The clearest example of a need to draw the line at "some point" is setting the voting age. Here, the law is inflexible; it would be administratively impossible to base voting eligibility on any factor other than an arbitrary demarcation. Laurence Tribe has located the following translation from Ihering's *Der Geist Das Roemischen* (1883) which discusses the absurdity of a voting right based on individual worthiness:

Take the example of civil and political personal capacity (majority and electoral right). Suppose that a legislator wishes to regulate this legally, and he comes forth with this idea: he who has the judgment and stability of character required to regulate his own affairs will be of full age; he who possesses the capacity and wishes to contribute to the good of the state will be an eligible elector. As just as this idea is, it would be absurd to institute it at all in abstract form, as one would suffer infinite pains to determine in each case the existence of these conditions. . . . the most irreproachable application of this law would not be safe from the objection of partiality. . . . How can the legislator avoid this stumbling block? Instead of these conditions he will fix others . . . which have the advantage over them of being more easily and surely recognized in a concrete manner; for example, the attainment of 25 years of age for majority; the possession of a certain wealth, the practice of certain professions, etc., for the right of elector. . . . this abandonment of a more exact hypothesis in an abstract form, in favor of a less exact and less adequate one more easily recognized in practice, is required by one of the law's own purposes—by the desirability of facility and certainty in its functioning. It is possible here and there in applying this law that mistakes will occur, that majority or electoral rights will be granted or refused in particular cases where they would not be under the abstract terms; yet this concrete mode of procedure is nonetheless preferable, in view of the necessities of life. (1975:14)

This is the prevailing argument in support of an inflexible rule on majority or maturity.

The line between legal minority and adulthood is set at the age of 18 in most states; in the others at 19 or 21. Many people call this division "artificial and simplistic," claiming that it obscures the dramatic differences among children of different ages and the striking similarities between older children and adults. If we look closely at the areas of law involving minors' rights, however, the law does not seem so rigid and inflexible as the use of an arbitrary dividing line would suggest. With the notable exception of the voting age, in almost every instance of a law that affects minors, some allowance is made for a "maturity factor"—that is, cases in which minors display a degree of maturity consistent with their desire to free themselves from the bonds of their minority status.

EMANCIPATION STATUTES

Judicial recognition of the maturity factor dates back to the nineteenth century and the doctrine of the emancipation of minors. Even then, the age of maturity was a flexible concept. Courts did not impose a rigid standard, but allowed parents to decide when their child was ready for independence (Katz et al. 1973). For example, in a case heard in the Vermont Supreme Court a 14-year-old boy sued to secure his own wages free from his father's creditors. The creditors contended that the boy was "too young" to be emancipated, but the court held that the father's prior acts had served to emancipate the boy despite his age. No law or policy prohibited early emancipation, and parents were not discouraged from "letting go" (Marks 1974).

The emancipation doctrine is dormant but not dead. It is unlikely that it will be revived in disputes over children's wages, but there are many situations today to which the concept of emancipation might be usefully applied. Consider, for example, the case of a 16- or 17-year-old, able to be employed and to live apart from parental supervision, who is locked in a disciplinary struggle with his or her father or mother. The struggle often brings such a child into court, where the tendency is to make him a ward of the state in a youth home or training school. Why not emancipate the child? The age of majority, which may be only months away, is all that stands between his freedom and his disruptive battle with his parents. Emancipation could bring an end to the struggle, freeing the parents of the duty to support and the child of the duty to obey. California, for example, has adopted a statute that considers emancipated

a minor 15 years or older who is living separate and apart from his parents or legal guardian, whether with or without consent of a parent or guardian, and regardless of the duration of such separate residence, and who is managing his own financial affairs, regardless of the source of his income. (Civil Code No. 64)

During his early years, a child has no desire to extricate himself from his parents' care, control, and supervision; rather he seeks out the relationship. The time comes, however, when he wishes to feel free from his parents. This time comes earlier for some children than for others, and is experienced with differing intensities. If the desire for separation comes before the age of majority, and the child is mature enough to be able to care for himself, there is some flexibility in the law, through the concept of emancipation, that could solve the problem.

LABOR LAWS

As already noted, restrictions on a minor's ability to be gainfully employed may severely restrict his autonomy. Child labor laws, however, allow considerable room for the maturity factor. Although the typical regulation states that no minor under 16 years of age "shall be permitted or allowed to work in, about, or in connection with any gainful employment at any time," most child labor laws make exceptions. For example:

> Minors between the ages of 14 and 16 to be employed outside school hours and during school vacations, but not in factories or hazardous occupations
> Minors 12 years of age and older who secure a certificate from the Department of Labor to be employed outside school hours in the sale and distribution of newspapers, magazines, and periodicals
> Minors of any age to be employed in domestic or farm work performed under the direction or authority of the minor's parent or guardian.

DRIVING

Most states allow for the licensing of persons between the ages of 16 and 18 if their parents sign the applications and they satisfactorily complete driver's education courses. Generally, the Division of Motor Vehicles is further authorized to issue a learner's permit to a person at least 15 years of age, which allows the minor to drive in the company of a parent or other licensed driver. Persons 14 years of age and older are often permitted to drive "road machines, farm tractors, and motor driven implements of husbandry" on state highways; there is no age restriction for operating such vehicles on highways adjacent to the land on which a person lives if he is engaged in farming operations.

TORT LAW AND CRIMINAL LAW

Juries are permitted to consider the maturity of the tort defendant in determining the extent to which he is held accountable for the damage. In the juvenile justice process, the old approach of recognizing stages of childhood development through the three "seven-year" presumptions has been discarded as inappropriate for the rehabilitative model, where a finding of "guilt" or "innocence" is not made. However, the maturity factor is now recognized in some new ways.

First, there are age limits on juvenile court jurisdiction in all states. The maximum age of such jurisdiction is the age of majority in more than half of the states, i.e., to be tried as a juvenile a person must be under the age of 18. In some states, however, the maximum age is set at 15 or 16.

Minimum age limits are rarely found in modern juvenile statutes. This is largely because jurisdiction extends to dependency and neglect cases as well as to delinquency cases, and dependency and neglect jurisdiction must extend to the youngest children.

A few states limit the definition of delinquency by a reference to age. In New York, for example, a delinquent is defined as a person between the ages of 7 and 16 who has committed an act that, if committed by an adult, would constitute a crime. When no age minimum is set, the common law criminal infancy defense, that no one under the age of 7 is capable of committing a crime, may be used to contest juvenile court jurisdiction. Some courts refuse to allow this defense on the ground that it does not apply to the civil delinquency proceeding, but other courts have allowed the defense to defeat juvenile jurisdiction (ALI/ABA 1977).

Second, the maturity factor plays a role in juvenile proceedings in the "transfer" or "waiver" process. This process, operative in all states except New York, provides for certain children to be referred to adult criminal court (ALI/ABA 1977). Most states set a minimum age for transfer, varying from 10 to 16. In theory, transfer is the device available to the courts to deal with certain situations in which a minor's case would be more appropriately handled in the criminal court. Its advocates claim that some children are so vicious and hardened, or have performed acts of such shocking criminality, that they are completely unamenable to treatment.

The transfer decision is based, in a sense, on the maturity factor. It may seem strange to equate maturity and hardened criminality, but it is fair to say that a certain kind of maturity—a loss of innocence and youthful malleability—is involved in the transfer decision.

CAPACITY TO CONTRACT AND CONSENT

Increasingly, the law allows for the maturity factor in the area of capacity and competency limitations: contract, marriage, and consent to medical treatment.

The "mature minor" rule is a long recognized exception to the general capacity limitation of minors in the law of contracts. If a minor, close to majority and having the appearance of an adult, enters into a contract, the person with whom he contracts is entitled to rely on his appearance and to assume that he is an adult. The minor will not be permitted to disaffirm the contract later. This rule is incorporated in statutes in some states, in others it has simply been adopted as a matter of common law (Murray 1974). In the case of educational laws, at least five states have adopted the Minor Student Capacity to Borrow Act, allowing 16-year-olds to sign for their own college loans.

Limitations on the age of marriage also make allowances for maturity. Persons under the age of majority, but 15 or older, are permitted to marry in most states with parental consent; some states allow underaged persons to obtain judicial approval of the marriage without parental consent, if the court believes the minor is mature.

Minors are deemed incapable of giving informed consent for medical treatment; the consent of someone legally authorized is necessary. If a physician renders medical care to a minor without such consent, he is in danger of a civil suit by the parent for assault and battery or for malpractice (for performing an unauthorized operation). If the parent withholds consent for surgery deemed necessary to save a minor's life, physicians have often refused to proceed without court authorization on behalf of the child.

In recent years, many states, recognizing the increased sophistication or maturity of modern teenagers, and in response to pressure from physicians, have adopted statutes reducing the age at which a minor can consent to medical care, and almost every state makes some allowance for the maturity factor in this area. Eleven states have enacted comprehensive statutes enabling minors to consent to medical care. Twelve states have codified the common law "emergency" exception. Statutes in twenty-one states permit married and/or pregnant minors to consent to their own medical care. The "mature minor" rule has also been recognized by statute in a number of states.

Many states have enacted legislation enabling minors to consent to medical care in certain specified situations, such as the detection, prevention, and treatment of venereal disease, pregnancy, and alcohol or drug abuse. Today, every state has a law giving minors the right to consent for diagnosis and treatment of venereal disease.

The law does not take an entirely arbitrary approach to questions of minority status; neither does it adhere to an age-of-majority test regardless of extenuating circumstances. Nevertheless, in most cases in which the maturity factor has been recognized, the vehicle for releasing the minor has been some form of parental consent.

As we have seen, exceptions to the restrictions of a minor's right to drive, marry, and work depend on parental approval, as does common law emancipation. Minors are free to drink, smoke, and read obscene literature under parental supervision.

The two areas in which recognition of the maturity factor is given independently of parental involvement are capacity to contract and borrow, and responsibility for personal injury. In neither is it necessary to confront the doctrine of parental authority directly. A minor can be held liable in a contract or tort action without his parent's control and authority over him ever being challenged.

Interference with parental autonomy comes only as a result of the parent's conduct, not the child's. Parents lose custodial rights only when they themselves are found to have behaved in an extremely abusive or neglectful manner toward their children. When the state does intervene, as in the criminal law area, the parental role remains dominant, both in the assumptions of juvenile incapacity upon which the juvenile justice system rests, and in the state's undertaking of the benevolent role of *parens patriae*. When courts intervene to protect a minor from the state, as in the civil rights area, the issue of parent-child conflict is not raised, since in most cases there is an identity of interest between parent and child.

4

Minors' Abortion and Contraception Rights: Implications for Parental Authority

AGAINST a background of almost solid legal support for parental authority and autonomy, the Supreme Court decided a case in July 1976 which, according to some, raised "serious questions about the assumptions underlying the entire concept of minority status," and had "serious implications for the heretofore basic legal assumption that parents have not only the constitutionally sanctioned right, but also the heavy responsibility to protect, educate and influence the values of their children" (Hafen 1977). This was the case of *Planned Parenthood of Central Missouri vs. Danforth.*

ABORTION

The issue under consideration in *Danforth* was the constitutionality of a Missouri statute requiring an unmarried, minor, pregnant female to obtain the written consent of one parent or person *in loco parentis* prior to submitting to an abortion during the first twelve weeks of pregnancy—unless the abortion had been certified by a physician as necessary to preserve her life. The Court ruled that the "State may not impose a blanket provision . . . requiring the consent of a parent or person *in loco parentis* as a condition for abortion of an unmarried minor during the first 12 weeks of her pregnancy."

The Court reiterated its holding of *Roe vs. Wade,* the celebrated abortion case, that "for the stage prior to approximately the end of the first trimester, the abortion decision and its effectuation must be left to the medical judgment of the pregnant woman's attending physician, without interference from the State." This holding in *Roe* had been based on a "constitutional right of privacy" which the Court found "broad enough to encompass a woman's decision whether or not to terminate her pregnancy."

The Court then observed that while "[m]inors, as well as adults, are protected by the Constitution and possess Constitutional rights . . . , the State has somewhat broader authority to regulate the activity of children than adults." The Court therefore perceived that the question facing it was "whether there is any significant state interest in conditioning . . . [a minor's] abortion on the consent of a parent or person *in loco parentis. . . .*" It considered "one suggested interest," that of safeguarding the family unit and protecting parental authority. This argument was rejected.

The Court held that "the State does not have the constitutional authority to give a third party an absolute, and possibly arbitrary, veto over the decision of the physician and his patient to terminate the patient's pregnancy (during the first 12 weeks of pregnancy), regardless of the reason for withholding consent." Cognizant of the implications of this ruling on the issue of "parental consent," the Court was constrained to include the following qualification: "We emphasize that our holding . . . does not suggest that every minor, regardless of age or maturity, may give effective consent for termination of her pregnancy."

A closely related case, *Bellotti vs. Baird* ("Bellotti I"), was decided on the same day as *Danforth,* and in this decision the Court elaborated on the above qualification. In *Bellotti I,* the Court suggested that what it objected to in the statute under consideration in *Danforth* was its blanket "parental veto" over the abortion decision, leaving no room for "mature minors" or for minors whose best interest would be served by obtaining an abortion to do so without parental consent or consultation. On the question of whether a minor's constitutional right to an abortion might be restricted, the Court was inconclusive in *Bellotti I*, refusing to rule on the validity of the Massachusetts statute under consideration before the Massachusetts Supreme Court had construed the statute.

Although the opinion was "inconclusive" on this issue, the Court was careful to avoid committing itself as to where the line should be drawn on interference with the minor's right to an abortion: "[W]e need [not] determine what factors are impermissible or at what point review of consent and good cause in the case of a minor become unduly burdensome."

In light of these two decisions, one could conclude that while a "blanket" parental veto of the minor's abortion decision is considered unconstitutional, something short of the "blanket veto" might be acceptable. The United States Supreme Court reaffirmed this position in 1983 when it upheld a lower court decision declaring that a blanket parental veto for all minors under the age of 15 was unconstitutional (*Akron vs. Akron Center for Reproductive Health*).

IMPLICATIONS OF *DANFORTH, BELLOTTI,*
AND *MATHESON*

The importance of the *Danforth* and *Bellotti I* decisions lay in their implications for issues and questions beyond the specific "right to an abortion." In *Danforth*, the Supreme Court appeared to venture for the first time into the area of a legal conflict between parent and child, and in so doing, to suggest that a child may have constitutional rights of his own which override his parents' wishes.

Danforth was a skimpy opinion; it raised more questions than it answered. It was a ruling of potentially far-reaching implications, yet it barely discussed the issues it purported to decide. The part of the opinion dealing with parental consent was only a page long.

The first test of *Danforth*'s reach came in the *Parham* case, involving commitment of minors to state mental hospitals. Lawyers for J. R. and J. L. argued that *Danforth* marked a limitation on the "traditional rights of parents," and that the case indicated "how little deference to parents is appropriate when the child is exercising a constitutional right." The *Parham* Court's holding has already been discussed at length; the case upheld the traditional rights of parents. The Court disposed of *Danforth* handily by distinguishing it in two sentences:

> The basic situation [in *Danforth*] . . . was very different; [*Danforth*] . . . involved an absolute parental veto over the child's ability to obtain an abortion. Parents in Georgia in no sense have an absolute right to commit their children to state mental hospitals; the statute requires the superintendent of each regional hospital to exercise independent judgment as to the child's need for confinement.

This response, of course, ignored the plaintiff's major point in *Parham:* an adult could not have been committed against his will in Georgia merely because a hospital professional concluded that he should be; an adult would have been entitled to notice and hearing before such action could be taken. Moreover, even an adult could not have committed himself without a physician's approval. *Parham* is thus a very clear ruling upholding parental autonomy.

It was not until 1979 that the Supreme Court undertook a comprehensive discussion of the issues raised in *Danforth* and *Bellotti I*. This occurred when *Bellotti I* returned to the Supreme Court for a second time. *Bellotti vs. Baird* ("Bellotti II") was appealed to the Supreme Court after the Court had remanded *Bellotti I* to the lower court to allow it to obtain from the Supreme Judicial Court of Massachusetts an authoritative interpretation of the particular Massachusetts parental consent statute in question. The particulars of that statute were as follows:

> If the mother is less than eighteen years of age and has not married, the consent of both the mother and her parents [to an abortion to be performed on the mother] is required. If one or both of the mother's parents refuse such consent, consent may be obtained by order of a judge of the superior court for good cause shown, after such hearing as he deems necessary. Such a hearing will not require appointment of a guardian for the

mother. If one of the parents has died or has deserted his or her family, consent by the remaining parent is sufficient. If both parents have died or deserted their family, consent of the mother's guardian or other person having duties similar to a guardian, or any person who has assumed the care and custody of the mother is sufficient.

On remand, and after a comprehensive interpretation by the Supreme Judicial Court of Massachusetts, the federal district court had declared the statute unconstitutional, relying heavily on *Danforth*.

In reviewing the district court opinion, the United States Supreme Court took the opportunity to elaborate on its view of the law affecting the parent-child relationship in its most extensive discussion of that topic to date. Said the Court:

A child, merely on account of his minority, is not beyond the protection of the Constitution. As the Court said in *In re Gault,* "whatever may be their precise impact, neither the Fourteenth Amendment nor the Bill of Rights is for adults alone." This observation, of course, is but the beginning of the analysis. The Court long has recognized that the status of minors under the law is unique in many respects. As Mr. Justice Frankfurter aptly put it, "(c)hildren have a very special place in life which law should reflect. Legal theories and their phrasing in other cases readily lead to fallacious reasoning if uncritically transferred to determination of a State's duty toward children." The unique role in our society of the family, the institution by which "we inculcate and pass down many of our most cherished values, moral and cultural," . . . requires that constitutional principles be applied with sensitivity and flexibility to the special needs of parents and children. We have recognized three reasons justifying the conclusion that the constitutional rights of children cannot be equated with those of adults: the peculiar vulnerability of children; their inability to make critical decisions in an informed, mature manner; and the importance of the parental role in child-rearing.

The Court's concern for the vulnerability of children is demonstrated in its decisions dealing with minors' claims to constitutional protection against deprivations of liberty or property interests by the State. . . . Viewed together, our cases show that although children generally are protected by the same constitutional guarantees against governmental deprivations as are adults, the State is entitled to adjust its legal system to account for children's vulnerability and their needs for "concern, . . . sympathy, and parental attention."

Second, the Court has held that the States validly may limit the freedom of children to choose for themselves in the making of important, affirmative choices with potentially serious consequences. These rulings have been grounded in the recognition that, during the formative years of childhood and adolescence, minors often lack the experience, perspective, and judgment to recognize and avoid choices that could be detrimental to them. . . .

Third, the guiding role of parents in the upbringing of their children justified limitations on the freedom of minors. The State commonly protects its youth from adverse governmental action and from their own immaturity by requiring parental consent to or involvement in important decisions by minors. But an additional and more important justification for state deference to parental control over children is that "(t)he child is not the mere creature of the State; those who nurture him and direct his destiny have the right, coupled with the high duty, to recognize and prepare him for additional obligations." "The duty to prepare the child for 'additional obligations' . . . must be read to include the inculcation of moral standards, religious beliefs, and elements of good citizenship." This affirmative process of teaching, guiding, and inspiring by precept and example is essential to the growth of young people into mature, socially responsible citizens.

We have believed in this country that this process, in large part, is beyond the competence of impersonal political institutions. Indeed, affirmative sponsorship of particular ethical, religious, or political beliefs is something we expect the State *not* to attempt in a society constitutionally committed to the ideal of individual liberty and freedom of choice.

Unquestionably, there are many competing theories about the most effective way for parents to fulfill their central role in assisting their children on the way to responsible adulthood. While we do not pretend any special wisdom on this subject, we cannot ignore that central to many of these theories, and deeply rooted in our nation's history and tradition, is the belief that the parental role implies a substantial measure of authority over one's children. Indeed, "constitutional interpretation has consistently recognized that the parents' claim to authority in their own household to direct the rearing of their children is basic to the structure of our society."

Properly understood, then, the tradition of parental authority is not inconsistent with our tradition of individual liberty; rather, the former is one of the basic presuppositions of the latter. Legal restrictions on minors, especially those supportive of the parental role, may be important to the child's chances for the full growth and maturity that make eventual participation in a free society meaningful and rewarding. Under the Constitution, the State can "properly conclude that parents and others, teachers, for example, who have [the] primary responsibility for children's well-being are entitled to the support of laws designed to aid discharge of that responsibility."

In spite of this very strong endorsement of the doctrine of parental autonomy, however, the Supreme Court in *Bellotti II* affirmed the district court and held the Massachusetts statute unconstitutional. The opinion went out of its way to endorse generally the state's right to require parental consultation and consent on many issues affecting minors:

Parental notice and consent are qualifications that typically may be imposed by the State on a minor's right to make important decisions. As immature minors often lack the ability to make fully informed choices that take account of both immediate and long-range consequences, a State reasonably may determine that parental consultation often is desirable and in the best interest of the minor.

Nevertheless, the Court disapproved of the parental consultation requirement in the *Bellotti* statute, and upheld the lower court's invalidation of the statute on grounds that the statute required a minor to seek her parents' consent *before* she was entitled to court relief. The Supreme Court ruled that the law was unconstitutional in two respects: it required parental consultation or notification in every instance and it permitted a judge to deny an abortion to a minor found by the court to be mature and fully competent to make the abortion decision. This, the Court ruled, was tantamount to an absolute veto exercised by the state and thus was impermissible under *Danforth*.

Danforth is further illuminated in the 1981 decision in *H. L. vs. Matheson,* a case involving the constitutionality of a Utah statute requiring a physician to "notify, if possible" the parents of a dependent, unmarried minor girl prior to performing an abortion on her.

The Court's opinion in *Matheson,* upholding the statute, was very narrow. It excluded from consideration "mature emancipated minors" because, the Court said, the minor in *Matheson* had not alleged in her complaint that she was either mature or emancipated. The Court relied heavily on that language from *Danforth* which appeared to leave room for states to impose some restrictions on minors: "our holding . . . does not suggest that every minor, regardless of age or maturity, may give effective consent for termination of her pregnancy." Since the plaintiff in *Matheson* failed to allege her maturity, she failed to bring herself within that class of minors qualified to challenge the statute on constitutional grounds; thus the statute, as applied to H. L., was not unconstitutional. There was a strong dissent from three justices pointing out that requiring notice was tantamount to requiring consent, and a concurring opinion by Justice Powell which underscored the narrowness of a ruling based on the technicalities of the plaintiff's failure to allege maturity in her complaint and the fact that the majority opinion left open the question whether the Utah statute could constitutionally apply to a "mature minor or a minor whose best interest would not be served by parental notification."

Do *Danforth*, *Bellotti I* and *II*, and *Matheson* signify a shift away from the law's heretofore solid support for the doctrine of parental autonomy?

The Court's reasoning in *Danforth* suggests some willingness to back away from a total endorsement of parental autonomy. The Court almost made light of the "suggested interest" of "protecting parental authority":

It is difficult . . . to conclude that providing a parent with absolute power to overrule a determination, made by the physician and his minor patient to terminate the patient's pregnancy, will serve to strengthen the family unit. Neither is it likely that such veto power will enhance parental authority or control where the minor and the nonconsenting parent are so fundamentally in conflict and the very existence of the pregnancy already has fractured the family structure. Any independent interest the parent may have in the termination of the minor daughter's pregnancy is no more weighty than the right of privacy of the competent minor mature enough to have become pregnant.

Logically extended, this argument could have far-reaching implications for other, not unusual, parent-child conflicts. Suppose a 15-year-old wishes to leave home and travel to Alaska. His parents forbid him from leaving; he leaves anyway, and his parents call in the police. The police arrest the child and bring him home to his parents as a runaway. The minor then "hires" a civil rights lawyer and challenges this infringement of the right of citizens to travel. Should the court rule that a parent does not have the right to stop his child from traveling to Alaska? It seems just as unlikely in this case as in *Danforth* that "providing the parent with absolute power to overrule the minor's determination [to travel] will serve to strengthen the family unit." Is it more likely in this case than it was in *Danforth* that supporting the parent will "enhance parental authority"? Cannot the very fact that the child has run away be taken to mean that the "family structure is already fractured"?

To take another example, let us consider a case of conflict over a minor's desire to marry. The Supreme Court has held on several occasions that "marriage is a basic civil right of man." The marriage laws of all states, however, establish a minimum age of marriage; this usually corresponds to the age of majority, but most states provide for marriage at a younger age "with parental consent." Consider the case of a teenager who can think of nothing but marrying his tenth-grade classmate and sweetheart. When he attempts to obtain the marriage license, he is told that he needs parental consent. His parents refuse. Driven by passion, he and his sweetheart drive to a neighboring state where the marriage is permitted, and there they marry. Upon their return home, his parents seek to have the marriage annulled. The minor challenges his parents' right to annul the marriage on constitutional grounds. Hasn't the fact that the boy married against his parents' wishes "already fractured the family structure"? Can it be construed as "strengthening the family unit" for the court to uphold the parents' right to annul the marriage? Will this holding strengthen parental authority?

In almost every case of parent-child conflict, the very fact that one party, whether it be parent or child, has resorted to the legal process indicates that parental authority has broken down and the family structure is fractured. The Court has been holding forth with eloquence for decades on the concept of family autonomy and parental authority. Does *Danforth* imply that at the moment an actual parent-child conflict first presents itself, the state's interest in upholding parental authority suddenly evaporates? There may, in fact, be a degree of realism in such a stance. If this reading of *Danforth* is extended, however, the concept of parental authority as a legal proposition becomes a paper tiger. Obviously, when a parent has to use the police, or the courts, or even a statutory parental consent requirement, to enforce his authority, there is little likelihood that his authority can be effectively established in the home.

A number of special factors must be weighed in considering the implications of the *Danforth* line of cases for the law of parent-child relations. First, it must be repeated that no direct parent-child conflict was at issue in any of these cases. Had a direct parent-child conflict been presented in *Danforth*, it is doubtful that the Court would have disposed so easily of the state's interest in upholding parental authority. The Court might have been presented with a case in which the parents had deep anti-abortion convictions which conflicted with the beliefs and wishes of their daughter. At the same time, these parents might have enjoyed a loving and supportive relationship with their daughter, and have made arrangements for the care of the child to be born. In such a case, it would be difficult for the Court to make sweeping statements pronouncing that the very existence of the pregnancy already has "fractured family structure." The Court, in weighing the cost to the daughter of requiring her to carry the child to term, might well come down in favor of abortion. But it would be a callous Court that would not be deeply troubled by its involvement in the conflict between the girl and her parents over such an emotionally charged issue.

Second, it must be remembered that all four cases involved direct attacks on a state statute—not a parent. It was the states of Missouri, Massachusetts, and Utah, not any parent, standing in the way of the minor's obtaining an abortion in those cases. Physicians were prohibited by state law from performing abortions without written parental consent. Whereas parental opposition might pose an obstacle to abortion even in states without such a statute, there is no question that the states of Missouri, Massachusetts, and Utah sought to impose an additional obstacle through their statutes.

Moreover, in each case the state was indirectly expressing its opposition to abortion, by singling it out among medical procedures. Indeed, each state had special legislation allowing minors to consent to certain other types of medical treatment.

The possibility must be considered that the *Danforth* line of cases are direct responses to what the Court saw as deliberate attempts to thwart the effect of *Roe vs. Wade*, and that the Court has merely carved out a special exception to the doctrine of parental autonomy in the reproductive rights area. This interpretation would not be inconsistent with the Court's previous decisions in the family planning/abortion area, where one finds repeated examples of the Court's impatience with legislative policies that are antagonistic to family planning efforts.

CONTRACEPTION

Griswold vs. Connecticut was the first case to reach the Supreme Court which involved a dispute centering on a state's pro-natalist policies. In *Griswold,* the Court ruled unconstitutional a Connecticut statute that made the use of contraceptives a criminal offense. The plaintiffs were physicians who prescribed contraceptives for their married patients. The Court based its opinion on a "new" right which it found to be implied by the Constitution: the right of marital privacy. Such a right is not specifically mentioned in the Bill of Rights, but was found to be included in the "penumbras, formed by emanations from the specific guarantees of the Bill of Rights." The *Griswold* opinion was a remarkable judicial decision; there was, in actuality, very little in the Bill of Rights upon which to base such a right. Justice Stewart's dissent is illuminating on this point:

I think this is an uncommonly silly law. . . . But we are not asked in this case to say whether the law is unwise or even asinine. We are asked to hold that it violates the United States Constitution. And that I cannot do.

Justice Stewart's opinion that the Connecticut law was "silly" probably comes very close to revealing the true reasons for the Court's ruling as it did, but of course the Court could never openly admit such a motive for its decision in the majority opinion (cf. Moynihan 1979:31). There the justices felt it necessary to shade themselves in the penumbra of the Bill of Rights.

Shortly after the *Griswold* decision was handed down in June 1965, the Massachusetts state legislature enacted a statute making it a felony for anyone to give away any article for the prevention of conception, except in the case of a registered physician prescribing a contraceptive for a married person or a registered pharmacist disbursing the prescribed medication. William Baird was convicted under this statute of giving an unmarried adult woman a package of vaginal foam. The case, *Eisenstadt vs. Baird,* was decided by the Supreme Court in 1972. The state of Massachusetts argued that the right of marital privacy found in the *Griswold* case did not apply to Baird's case, as it protected only married people.

Massachusetts sought to justify the statute on the grounds that it served valid state purposes. The Court reviewed these alleged purposes using its most lenient standard of review—that of judging whether the statute is "rationally related to a valid public purpose." In general, it has been impossible for those wishing to set aside state legislation to overcome the rational relationship test in constitutional challenges. In *Eisenstadt,* however, the Court simply refused to believe that the statute served a valid state purpose. First, the state argued that the purpose of the statute was to discourage premarital sexual intercourse, and the Court responded:

We cannot agree that the deterrence of premarital sex may reasonably be regarded as the purpose of the Massachusetts law. . . . It would be plainly unreasonable to assume that Massachusetts has prescribed pregnancy and the birth of an unwanted child as punishment for fornication, which is a misdemeanor under Massachusetts General Laws. . . . Aside from the scheme of values that assumption would attribute to the state, it is abundantly clear that the effect of the ban on distribution of contraceptives to unmarried persons has at best a marginal relation to the proffered objective. . . . The rationality of this justification is dubious, particularly in light of the admitted widespread availability to all persons . . . unmarried as well as married, of birth control devices for the prevention of disease, as distinguished from the prevention of contraception. . . . Nor, in making contraceptives available to married persons without regard to their intended use, does Massachusetts attempt to deter married persons from engaging in illicit sexual relations with unmarried persons. Even on the assumption that the fear of pregnancy operates as a deterrent to fornication, the Massachusetts statute is thus so riddled with exceptions that deterrence of premarital sex cannot reasonably be regarded as its aim. . . . Fornication is a misdemeanor, entailing a thirty dollar fine, or three months in jail. Violation of the present statute is a felony, punishable by five years in prison. We find it hard to believe that the legislature adopted a statute carrying a five-year penalty for its possible, obviously by no means fully effective, deterrence of the commission of a ninety-day misdemeanor. . . . We cannot believe that in this instance Massachusetts has chosen to expose the aider and abetter who simply *gives away* a contraceptive to 20 times the 90 day sentence of the offender himself . . . such deterrence cannot reasonably be taken as the purpose of the ban on distribution of contraceptives to unmarried persons.

The state also suggested that the statute served a health regulatory purpose by "controlling the distribution of potentially harmful articles." Again the Court simply refused to believe this reasoning:

It is plain that Massachusetts had no such purpose in mind before the enactment of . . . the statute. . . . Consistent with the fact that the statute was contained in a chapter dealing with "Crimes Against Chastity, Morality, Decency and Good Order," it was cast only in terms of morals. A physician was forbidden to prescribe contraceptives even when needed for the protection of health. . . . Nor . . . do we believe that the legislature suddenly reversed its field and developed an interest in health. Rather it merely made what it thought to be the precise accommodation necessary to escape the *Griswold* ruling. . . . If health were the rationale, the statute would be both discriminatory and overbroad. . . . If there is need to have a physician prescribe . . . contraceptives, that need is as great for unmarried persons as for married persons. . . . If the prohibition is to be taken to mean that the same physician who can prescribe for married patients does not have sufficient skill to protect the health of patients who lack a marriage certificate, or who may be currently divorced, it is illogical to the point of irrationality. . . . We conclude that, despite the statute's superficial earmarks as a health measure, health, on the face of the statute, may no more reasonably be regarded as its purpose than the deterrence of premarital sexual relations.

The "rational relationship" test does not normally justify such a rigorous scrutiny of the consistency among various parts of a legislative scheme. Both prior to *Eisenstadt,* and since then as well, the Court's rulings that a statute need only pass the rational relationship test has been a virtual guarantee that the legislation would be upheld. In *Eisenstadt,* the Court was plainly ready to believe that the Massachusetts legislature was openly hostile to birth control and prepared to strike down such measures to the fullest extent possible under *Griswold.*

The Court then considered whether the state of Massachusetts could constitutionally adopt a policy prohibiting contraception.

. . . "Whatever the rights of the individual to access to contraceptives may be, the rights must be the same for unmarried and the married alike."

If under *Griswold* the distribution of contraceptives to married persons cannot be prohibited, a ban on distribution to unmarried persons would be equally impermissible . . . in *Griswold* the right of privacy in question inhered in the marital relationship. Yet the marital couple is not an independent entity with a mind and heart of its own, but an association of two individuals each with a separate intellectual and emotional make-up. If the right of privacy means anything, it is the right of the *individual,* married or single, to be free from unwarranted governmental intrusion into matters so fundamentally affecting a person as the decision whether to bear or beget a child. . . . The state could not, consistently with the Equal Protection Clause, outlaw distribution to unmarried but not to married persons. In each case the evil, as perceived by the State, would be identical, and the underinclusion would be invidious.

It is impossible to pinpoint from this language precisely what the Court's constitutional reasoning was for holding that Massachusetts could not prohibit the distribution of contraceptives to single persons, in view of the fact that *Griswold*'s holding was based on *marital* privacy, not sexual privacy or even individual privacy.

REPRODUCTIVE RIGHTS

The Court's apparent determination to remove all barriers to individual access to services to control reproductive capacity emerged in full force in *Roe vs. Wade.* This case presented a more difficult problem for the Court; it was forced to deal with the question of when life begins, and to choose between saving a fetus and the mother's well-being. The issues in *Roe* are extremely complex and are beyond the scope of this book. *Roe* was clearly a victory for reproductive rights, however, and abortion is an essential back up when contraception fails or is unobtainable. Removal of the barriers to abortion as a birth control measure was crucial to the family planning movement. From the standpoint of constitutional law, however, *Roe* was another bombshell that left some constitutional law scholars spinning. In their view, the decision could not be explained in terms of traditional constitutional law doctrine; it was the most striking case yet of "judicial legislation."

The *Griswold, Eisenstadt,* and *Roe* cases make sense if they are viewed simply as contraception/abortion cases and if no effort is made to fit them into the overall scheme of constitutional law theory. Such a cavalier approach is open only to those of us who do not profess to be expert in the theory of constitutional law, but the possibility that the Court has assumed a policy-making role in this area must nevertheless be considered. It is in fact true that the much-heralded implications of each of these cases for other areas of constitutional law are yet to be fulfilled. The Court has not extended the *Griswold/Eisenstadt* right to privacy to any other area of sexual behavior. *Griswold*-based challenges to sodomy, fornication, and adultery statutes have all failed. The Court has not extended its equal protection analysis in *Eisenstadt* to any other area in which discrimination on the basis of marital status occurs.

Likewise, the Court's rulings in *Danforth, Bellotti,* and *Matheson* probably do not signify any shift in the law of parent-child relations generally. Instead, the Court appears to view abortion and contraception as a special area. The language of *Bellotti II* strongly suggests this kind of special treatment. After a ringing defense of parental autonomy, the Court said:

> But we are concerned here with a constitutional right to seek an abortion. The abortion decision differs in important ways from other decisions that may be made during minority. The need to preserve the constitutional right and the unique nature of the abortion decision, especially when made by a minor, require a State to act with particular sensitivity when it legislates to foster parental involvement in this matter.
>
> The pregnant minor's options are much different from those facing a minor in other situations, such as deciding whether to marry. A minor not permitted to marry before the age of majority is required simply to postpone her decision. She and her intended spouse may preserve the opportunity for later marriage should they continue to desire it. A pregnant adolescent, however, cannot preserve for long the possibility of aborting, which effectively expires in a matter of weeks from the onset of pregnancy.
>
> Moreover, the potentially severe detriment facing a pregnant woman is not mitigated by her minority. Indeed, considering her probable education, employment skills, financial resources, and emotional maturity, unwanted motherhood may be exceptionally burdensome for a minor. In addition, the fact of having a child brings with it adult legal responsibility, for parenthood, like attainment of the age of majority, is one of the traditional criteria for the termination of the legal disabilities of minority. In sum, there are few situations in which denying a minor the right to make an important decision will have consequences so grave and indelible.
>
> Yet, an abortion may not be the best choice for the minor. The circum-

stances in which this issue arises will vary widely. In a given case, alternatives to abortion, such as marriage to the father of the child, arranging for its adoption, or assuming the responsibilities of motherhood with the assured support of family, may be feasible and relevant to the minor's best interests. Nonetheless, the abortion decision is one that simply cannot be postponed, or it will be made by default with far-reaching consequences.

For these reasons, "the State may not impose a blanket provision . . . requiring the consent of a parent or person *in loco parentis* as a condition for abortion of an unmarried minor during the first 12 weeks of her pregnancy." Although such deference to parents may be permissible with respect to other choices facing a minor, the unique nature and consequences of the abortion decision make it inappropriate "to give a third party an absolute, and possibly arbitrary, veto over the decision of the physician and his patient to terminate the patient's pregnancy, regardless of the reason for withholding consent."

PARENTAL AUTONOMY

Even if *Danforth* and *Bellotti II* are seen as departures from or exceptions to the general law of parental autonomy, they have not strayed very far. Although *Matheson* involved parental notification rather than parental consent, the case still focused attention on the "mature minor" language in *Danforth* and *Bellotti II,* and both the Court's opinion and the concurring opinion suggest strongly that the right to decide whether to have an abortion is to be extended only to mature minors and those who can show that an abortion without their parents' knowledge is in their best interest. Such a limitation would leave the law largely where it stood before *Danforth,* solid in its support for parental autonomy, and in its emphasis on minors' incompetence, with exceptions made only for "mature" minors. It remains to be seen whether Justice Powell's position, set out in his concurring opinion in *Matheson,* will prevail: that exceptions should also be made in the abortion area when there is a finding that the abortion would be in the minor's best interest. This would be a step away from parental autonomy, since the law generally presumes that a parent whose parental rights are intact and not questioned knows what is in the child's best interest.

There are still other reasons why *Danforth, Bellotti,* and *Matheson* may not have significant impact on the general law of parent-child relations. The concept of parental autonomy is firmly rooted in American jurisprudence. Furthermore, the consensus is that the state has failed miserably in its efforts to assume a parental role in caring for children. The thrust of the "social work" movement today is toward providing as much support as possible to parents in their child-rearing tasks. No reliable substitute has been found for the parent, and the state still seeks to support parents in every possible way.

LIMITS OF ADJUDICATION

The advocates of children's liberation have not been enthusiastically received by the majority of our populace, and it is unlikely that the courts, one of our most conservative institutions, will take up the banner of children's liberation in the near future. Nor are the courts eager to increase their caseloads. The entire thrust of judicial reform is toward a reduction in caseload, particularly in the area of family controversies which are not hopeful prospects for judicial resolution. Though these controversies may sometimes focus on a single issue about which the law has expressed an opinion, the legal battle usually just scratches the surface of a very deep and complex family problem that may have a long history. There is little that can be done in a court of law truly to resolve such a dispute, and the courts are painfully aware of this reality.

Parent-child disputes are especially unlikely to be resolved through adjudication. The parent-child relationship, for better or for worse, is endlessly complex and constantly changing; it survives the death of the parent, and it influences every other relationship in the child's life. What can a judge say from his superficial perspective that will have a meaningful effect on such a bond? Moreover, as the Supreme Court said in *Bellotti II,* parent-child disputes also contain an element that is often missing in other family-centered disputes, the capacity for self-resolution. Eventually the minor will be an adult and any aspect of the battle that could be solved through the legal process will be resolved by the child's attaining majority. In many cases, this will happen in the time it would take a case to wind its way through the courts.

Viewed from this perspective—that of the incipient capability of many parent-child disputes for self-resolution—the abortion cases truly can be set apart from the typical parent-child controversy. As the Court noted in *Bellotti II*, the capacity for self-resolution is not operative in an abortion case: the decision cannot wait even a matter of months; it must be made quickly.

PART TWO

THE SOCIAL AND PSYCHOLOGICAL BACKGROUND

5

The Development
of Competence

WHEN do adolescents become competent to make important decisions without the guidance and supervision of adults? In particular, when are they sufficiently mature to make independent decisions about contraception and abortion? These are both scientific and policy questions. If psychological and sociological research on adolescent competence could answer them precisely, policymakers would have an easy task. Unfortunately, the research is both sparse and generalized; only approximate answers can be given to questions about adolescent competence. But even approximate answers can serve as guidelines for policymakers.

Much has been published about adolescents; at least one article about "teenagers" can usually be found in the magazine rack at the supermarket check-out counter or at the newsstand. Unfortunately, these articles are impressionistic and speculative and are rarely based on solid research findings. There have been few empirical studies of adolescence and fewer still of the competence of early adolescents. This situation is changing, as researchers begin to direct attention toward various aspects of adolescent development, but the empirical evidence they have produced permits us to formulate only tentative answers to the policy questions posed above.

We know, of course, that the development of competence takes place over time. Infants are dependent, at the mercy of others to meet their physical, social, and emotional needs. Adults, given normal development, are able to operate in a relatively autonomous manner. What happens between infancy and adulthood? Competent social human beings are created through the process of socialization. And it appears that the family, in one form or another, is universally involved in that process. But what is "competence," the quality that adults have derived from the socialization process and that we believe minors should demonstrate before being permitted to make important decisions on their own?

DEFINITIONS OF COMPETENCE

There is no single clear-cut definition of competence that encompasses everything we need to talk about. Researchers use several other terms interchangeably with the term *competence*—adaptation, mastery, coping, effectiveness, maturity. They also use the concept of competence variously. Some deal with competence as a general quality, some with competence in specific situations. Some focus on the individual's personality structure, some on the individual's general behavior in the environment, and some on the individual's social skills or role performance. Several examples will give an idea of the diverse definitions and uses. Diana Baumrind defines instrumental competence as "social responsibility, independence, achievement orientation, and vitality" (1973:4), with further definitions for each of these components. Heath (1977) considers competence a technical concept referring to adaptive effectiveness. Connolly and Bruner define competence as "intelligence in the broadest sense, operative intelligence [which is] *knowing how* rather than simply *knowing that*" (1974:3). For them, competence is being able to change the environment or adapt to it. M. Brewster Smith defines the competent self as comprising the belief that the self is effective in doing things in the world, with an attitude of hope toward the world because it can be changed by one's efforts: "With these positive attitudes toward self and world goes a characteristic behavioral orientation—that of pursuing realistic goals and challenges. This is, in effect, an active, coping orientation high in initiative, not a passive or defensive one characterized by very low goals . . . or unrealistically high ones." Smith continues : "Accompanying these dispositions of the self are the array of knowledge, habits, skills, and abilities that are required to translate hopeful expectations and active orientations into effective behavior" (1968:281–282). Lange, Ladd, and Davis, in discussing the nature and development of competent young children, conclude from theory and research that competence, be it social or intellectual, has an "operative" or "instrumental" quality (1982:4). The competent young child is the one who is becoming an active, self-motivated, and goal-oriented participant in dealing with his environment. Though all of these definitions differ, they reflect a common theme of active, effective participation in one's environment.

Other definitions abound. Robert D. Hess defines social competence as "behaviour which relates individuals to the institutions of the society in which they live" (1974:283). Baker (1982) suggests that social competence or cultural competence is the attainment of achieving a sense of social organization and social reality sufficient to make sense of things. This cultural competence operates on the level of one's personal theories of self and world as well as on the level of social behavior. For Foote and Cottrell, interpersonal competence "denotes capabilities to meet and deal with a changing world, to formulate ends and implement them" (1955:49). They elaborate six components of interpersonal competence: health, intelligence, empathy, autonomy, judgment, and creativity. Inkeles defines competence as "the ability effectively to attain and perform in three sets of statuses: Those which one's society will normally assign one, those in the repertoire of one's social system one may appropriately aspire to, and those which one might reasonably invent or elaborate for oneself" (1966:265).

Clearly, there is no obvious agreement within the social science community about what competence is. Different investigators are interested in different forms of competence and define it in terms of their own philosophies or research needs. We can nonetheless distinguish two basic kinds of competence among the wide variety of definitions. One has to do with the individual's cognitive or intellectual ability: what does he/she know, how rationally does he/she think, and how effectively does he/she solve problems or make decisions? A second has to do with the individual's ability to act in the social environment: How well does he carry out his plans, solutions, or decisions? How well does she perform her roles, how well does he communicate, how much influence does she have over others, how capable is he to make adaptations based on feedback received from others?

COGNITIVE COMPETENCE

Most research into adolescent cognitive development has been guided by a theory proposed by Jean Piaget, a Swiss psychologist who examined the nature and process of children's intellectual development. Piaget demonstrated that the thought of the young child is different in many ways from the thought of older children and adults. For example, young children are egocentric, considering themselves the center of the world, and expecting everyone else to see things as they do. As children grow older, they can begin to take the perspectives of others and to understand that there are various views of any event. Although Piaget's theory holds that development is continuous, it recognizes that development progresses through identifiable stages. A child begins with an elementary form of reasoning that requires actions and manipulation of concrete objects, through reasoning that is more reliant on the symbolic representation of concrete objects, to a form of reasoning that allows abstract and hypothetical thinking. This stage of logical or formal reasoning begins to emerge during early adolescence, at about age 11 or 12.

Since age is typically the legal criterion of competence, it is important to be as clear as possible about age in reporting psychological and sociological research findings. Social scientists occasionally divide adolescence into stages. Despite some variation in the range of ages included in each category, there is an approximate consensus that early adolescence is 12 and 13 years old, middle adolescence is 14 and 15, and late adolescence is 16 and older. Researchers do not agree about when adolescents become generally and consistently capable of logical, systematic reasoning. As examples of their varying conclusions, we will mention just a few research findings. Manaster (1977), summarizing research on logical reasoning and age, notes numerous studies suggesting that formal logic is reached in the late teens or early twenties. On the other hand, a research study involving 2,000 adolescents (Fitzgerald, Nesselroade, and Baltes 1973) shows that the organizational pattern of adult intelligence emerges prior to early adolescence. Yudin (1966) has posited that both age and intelligence are involved in the development of logical reasoning: significant gains occur in the adolescent of average intelligence from 12 to 14 years of age, in the adolescent of low intelligence from 14 to 16, and in the adolescent of high intelligence from before 12.

The conflicting evidence from these research studies makes it impossible to say that all adolescents attain cognitive competence by age 15, 16, or even 17. However, several research projects concerned with adolescents' developing competence to make decisions about medical treatment have consistently found that adolescents over 14 years of age are adultlike in their decisions about their own medical treatment. Although they do not directly measure levels of intellectual functioning, these studies suggest that in certain content areas adolescents exhibit adultlike competence in decision making.

One study tested the hypothesis that 14-year-olds do not differ from the persons defined by law as adults in the capacity to provide competent informed consent and refusal for medical and psychological treatment (Weithorn and Campbell 1982). The study compared the performance of subjects aged 9, 14, 18, and 21 on a measure developed to operationalize legal standards of competence. In general, 14-year-olds demonstrated adult levels of competency on four measures (evidence of choice, reasonable outcome, rational reasons, and understanding) for four hypothetical medical problems (diabetes, epilepsy, depression, and enuresis). Nine-year-olds, however, were less competent than adults in the areas of understanding and rational process. As interesting as these findings are, it is difficult to generalize from them since the subjects were healthy people considering hypothetical situations. Further research should investigate whether young people affected by psychological or physical disorders exhibit decreased cognitive abilities in health-care decision making or whether the reality of the situation enhances decision making.

The three legal requirements of fully informed consent are competency, knowledge, and volition. The Weithorn and Campbell study did not investigate developmental differences in adolescents' capacities to make "voluntary" health-care decisions; Grisso and Vierling (1978) did. They reviewed research on the developmental factors related to the capacity to provide informed consent, and concluded that at 15 years of age adolescents generally can make treatment decisions that are not unduly influenced by others. They point out, however, that there is still so little research evidence about what young people know, how they think, and how they respond in various clinical settings and health-care situations that conclusions must be tentative.

An assessment by Feshbach and Tremper (1981) of the attitudes of parents and adolescents toward health-care decisions by minors showed that, on many items, adolescents and their parents think young people are competent to make choices at ages generally younger than those usually permitted by law. Not unexpectedly, specified ages varied with content areas; for example, all groups specified much younger ages for TV-viewing decisions than for medical treatment decisions. Surprisingly, however, correspondences between parents and adolescents in the ages specified for each decision area were very close. Feshbach and Tremper suggest that a system in which legal autonomy began earlier and was phased in over a period of time would better reflect attitudes about adolescents' decision making than does the present system (see Bane 1976:111–112).

The emergence of political thought during early adolescence is another tangential research area concerned with the age of acquiring adultlike reasoning. Adelson and his colleagues (1972) have concluded that neither sex nor intelligence nor social class accounted for much of the variation in the growth of political concepts. The crucial variable was age. There is a profound shift in the character of political thought from ages 12 and 13 to ages 15 and 16. At the older ages there is a sharp decline of authoritarian views and a greater capacity for abstract and ideological thinking.

Research evidence does not permit us to specify an exact age at which adolescents become cognitively competent decision makers. But we can say with some assurance that the evidence supports our conclusion that the potential for logical reasoning and competent decision making is present during the middle-adolescent years.

We return to the qualification we made on that conclusion, that is, that the realization of that potential for cognitive competence is dependent upon many social environmental forces. Piaget (1972) has suggested that logical reasoning may not be unitary, that is, this stage of logical reasoning may not exist as an all-pervasive style of thinking. It may not be applied in all problem-solving situations. A person's interests, aptitudes and abilities, and learning experiences influence whether he applies logical reasoning in any given situation or to any given topic. The potential for competence in logical reasoning may be present in adolescence, perhaps at the age of 11 or 12, but the realization of that potential depends on specific learning experiences (Berzonsky 1978).

With this evidence comes the suggestion that adolescence, particularly early adolescence, may be a critical period for instruction and for much new learning (Berzonsky 1978). The educational implications here are obvious. Family life education, sex education, competence training, to give only a few examples, could be extremely important subject areas in late elementary and junior high-school courses. The suggestion has even been made that the very character of current education, with the student's often unquestioning dependence on the intellectual authority of the teacher, may retard the emergence of mature judgment (Peel 1971, 1975). Several investigators have offered research evidence that a greater opportunity for young adolescents to discuss and evaluate problems with peers and teachers might lead to an earlier development of intellectual maturity, especially in terms of social cognition which can be thought of as an understanding of one's social world (Enright 1976; Marsh, Serafica, and Barenboim 1980; Muuss 1982).

Because adolescents function cognitively within a social setting, changes in their cognitive development ought to be evident in their social behavior. David Elkind's writing (1967a, 1967b, 1974, 1978) provides a glimpse into some of the behaviors of the young adolescent that parents and others working with young people sometimes find troubling, and he suggests cognitive explanations for these behaviors. Elkind's research is illustrative of two points that seem relevant. First, it reveals that an adolescent's thought patterns are in a state of change. Adolescents sometimes find themselves reacting in unfamiliar ways to familiar situations. Because they are beginning to reflect upon their own thoughts and to take the perspective of others they now can see and understand differently from before. Second, the research shows us that because the young adolescent is in the process of becoming a competent individual, he or she needs a great deal of understanding and room to mature.

The four cognitive-behavioral phenomena that Elkind (1978) describes in some detail are *pseudostupidity, imaginary audience, personal fable,* and *apparent hypocrisy. Pseudostupidity,* the tendency to appear stupid when the adolescent is really quite bright, results from the new ability to conceive of alternatives while he/she has not yet developed the ability to assign priorities and to decide upon the most appropriate alternative. *Imaginary audience* results from the adolescent's growing awareness of other people's thoughts and opinions and his tendency to think that those around him are as preoccupied with his behavior and appearance as he is himself. As the young adolescent comes to understand that everyone has his/her own set of preoccupations, the influence of this imaginary audience diminishes. The phenomenon of *personal fable* is the belief in invulnerability, common to adolescents, exemplified by the statement "It won't happen to me." This provides a partial explanation for a young person's risk-taking—drugs, reckless driving, sexual experimentation, and so on. *Apparent hypocrisy,* very much like pseudostupidity, results from the adolescent's capacity to formulate general principles of behavior without necessarily having the ability to apply them to specific behaviors.

The egocentrism, evidenced by these cognitive-behavioral phenomena, that seems to be so common in adolescents, comes in large measure from their changing view of themselves and their relationships with other people. They begin to think differently about themselves, and their values, and their goals. This developing cognitive competence affects every area of their lives.

SOCIAL COMPETENCE

In addition to exploring the adolescent's cognitive competence—intellectual knowledge, logical thinking, and problem-solving skills—we also want to investigate the adolescent's social competence. How well does he or she navigate in social waters? How good are the social skills, communications skills, and interpersonal skills necessary for appropriate interaction with others, for drawing information from others, for having some influence over others, and for applying rational thinking to important social situations? For example, the level of cognitive competence in minors faced with problem pregnancies affects their awareness of the alternatives, their knowledge of where and how to get the information they need, and their ability to think rationally about their alternatives. Their level of social competence affects their ability to successfully communicate their need for additional information, to discuss their alternatives rationally with peers, parents, and perhaps other adults, and to implement their decisions (while, if necessary, maintaining their autonomy and independence in the face of pressures from others to follow a different course). This does not assume that any one decision is more rational than others. However a higher level of cognitive and social competence is more likely to lead to a better decision for the adolescent in question, and to the successful implementation of that decision.

The research literature on the social competence of early adolescents to make family-planning decisions is virtually nonexistent. So we must turn to a variety of studies of social competence regarding other issues, and with other age groups, in order to gain some understanding of what is involved.

There is a clear recognition among social scientists and clinicians of the importance of social competence (the ability to engage in satisfactory interpersonal relationships) both from the perspective of getting something done and of gaining personal satisfaction. Peterson suggests "that interpersonal behavior is more important than practically anything else one may examine in the entire domain of human existence" (1977:306). A focus on interpersonal relationships is found in many of the social sciences. In psychology, there is a growing emphasis upon studying behavior in its natural context. Bronfenbrenner (1979) expresses this in terms of human ecology. Others (Magnusson and Endler 1977; Howard 1982) emphasize the importance of interaction between person and situation, indicating that people are typically part of the situational context. In sociology, there is the same growing emphasis on processes of interaction. An emphasis on symbolic interaction (Blumer 1969; Meltzer and Manis 1978) goes back a long time, as does the emphasis on behavior in natural settings as expressed by the Chicago school (Wiley 1979; Faught 1980). But the current emphasis involves the careful study of sequences of interaction, studied at close range, in order to gain understanding of human behavior. This attempt to understand human behavior, and to explain it, is based on more detailed sequential and process information than had generally been gathered previously (Strauss 1978; Blalock and Wilken 1979; Scanzoni and Szinovacz 1980). It evolves from a belief in the importance of interpersonal interaction and negotiation in individual and group decision making as well as in the development of individual competence.

Many of the available studies of social competence focus on infants and young children and examine the repertoire of behavior they employ to meet their needs for food, comfort, and attention. This research is of limited relevance to the behavior of early adolescents in the family-planning area. We will therefore refer to only a few general accounts of such research. Bronson (1974) focused upon interaction, particularly communication, between mother and child, and referred to their "interactive competence," stressing that the mother's sensitivity to the baby's behavior and needs is crucial to the child's normal development. Dibble and Cohen (1974) also included measures of competence based on the relationship between parents and young children and stressed the interactivity between the relationship and the development of a child's social competence. Although this research deals with young children, the importance of the relationship between parent (or other caretaker) and child that it indicates carries through into adolescence, as we shall later see.

It is therefore essential, in assessing the social competence of children or adolescents, to look closely at the context within which their behavior occurs. It is only within that context that we can make an informed judgment about social competence—about whether the verbal or nonverbal behavior (Erickson and Schultz 1977) is appropriate for that context. Similarly, Rausch (1977), focusing on the interplay of person and situation, stresses the importance of the situation in understanding and explaining behavior and implies that, if the situation is ignored, judgments about social competence cannot be made.

The development of social competence takes place, by and large, within the family. For this reason, researchers have paid special attention to parental control and influence, the adolescent's bid for autonomy from the family, and parent-youth communications (see Rollins and Thomas, 1979).

PARENTAL INFLUENCE. One of these researchers is Diana Baumrind, who has carried out a series of studies of styles of parental control (1968, 1971, 1975, 1978a), relating these styles to the instrumental competence of early adolescents. (She considers instrumental competence, that is the ability to be socially responsible and socially effective, to be a type of social competence.) To Baumrind, social competence consists of such attributes as social responsibility, objectivity, self-control, independence, achievement orientation, and vigor. Socially responsible behavior is friendly, facilitative, and cooperative. Independence can be thought of as goal-oriented, self-determining behavior. Achievement orientation means seeking intellectual challenges and solving problems efficiently and deliberately (Baumrind 1978).

Early adolescents display social competence primarily through an ability to balance their responsibility to parents and their independence. Baumrind's work suggests that parents who are authoritative, who set rules and requirements, but do so rationally, with explanations and with attention to their children's desires, are more likely to rear socially competent children than are parents who are permissive or authoritarian. Forman and Forman (1981) concur; they have found that reasonable rules provide limits within which children can become genial, self-assured, and free from anxiety.

Another relevant study was carried out by McClelland et al. (1978) who interviewed and tested some of the people who had been studied as children by Sears, Maccoby, and Levin (*Patterns of Child Rearing* 1957). McClelland et al. were interesting in determining whether the different ways in which their respondents

had been brought up helped or hindered their achievement of social and moral maturity. The primary conclusion of the study was
that the major predictor of the highest levels of adult social and
moral maturity was not the child-rearing techniques parents had
employed during the first five years of this sample's childhood, but
the way the parents felt about their children. Those children whose
parents, especially the mothers, loved them reached the highest
levels of maturity.

There is suprisingly little developmental research on the differ-
ential effects of parental styles on adolescent autonomy. Questions
remain about parental styles, e.g., democratic vs. autocratic (Elder
1962:63), permissive, authoritarian, and authoritative (Baumrind
1971), for children of various ages, and about the differing influences of mothers and fathers. One investigation of adolescent autonomy (Enright et al. 1980) has, however, determined that, for
seventh and eleventh graders, gender is the most important variable: males generally had higher autonomy scores as measured by
the Kurtines scale (1978). The most likely explanation is that males
are encouraged to be assertive and autonomous while females are
rewarded for passivity and dependence. The studies by Enright et
al. point to the importance of sex-role socializaton as well as parenting style in the development of adolescent independence.

It is difficult to isolate the effects of parental influence because
parental influence itself is difficult to define and isolate. One approach is to measure parental influence by measuring the adolescent's acceptance or rejection of parental authority. Smith (1977)
studied 3,600 sixth- to twelfth-grade students and found that their
acceptance of parental authority was associated most strongly with
their perceptions that they received benefits from their parents and
that their parents were competent. This suggests that the "personal" relationship between parent and offspring is the most important determinant of a parent's success in controlling certain aspects of the child's behavior. A number of researchers have
determined that children have a healthy dependence upon their
parents when their parents are actively nurturing (e.g., Baumrind
1978a; Condry and Siman 1974; Jessor and Jessor 1974; Larson
1974; Smith 1971.)

Another way of assessing parental influence is measuring children's orientation. Several researchers have noted that children gradually shift their orientation from family to peers, and/or to themselves, but there is no clear evidence concerning the timing or degree of this change (Bowerman and Kinch 1969; Brittain 1967). Others have examined changes in parent-youth disagreement; they find no simple linear pattern of increasing or decreasing generational disagreement (Chand, Crider, and Willits 1975). Disagreement about items designated "youth-oriented behavior," such as hair styles and clothing styles, was found to be high; yet the data do not support the notion that youth reject parental norms. Parental opinions are clearly preferred to the opinions of friends, although the preference lessens during adolescence when there is a shift from parental influence.

Utech and Hoving (1969) administered a social dilemma questionnaire to children in grades three through eleven who were required to make decisions based on what their parents would say or on what their same-age friends would say. The study found that the proportion who conformed to parents rather than to peers decreased significantly with age. No sex differences were detected. Another study suggests that there are sex differences among adolescents in the influence of parents and peers on choices made. Emmerich (1978) found that in hypothetical situations in which an adolescent was faced with two alternatives, one favored by parents, the other by peers, males in the ninth grade chose parent-approved alternatives more often than did ninth-grade females or twelfth-grade males. The females' responses remained stable over the period. It seems that the relative influence of parents and peers is determined by the situation and by the sex of the adolescent. Further research will have to determine the reliability of sex differences as well as changes that occur with age. Larson (1972) studied seventh-, ninth-, and twelfth-graders and determined that the significance of a situation affected their choice of action more than did pressures from either their parents or their peers. His findings suggest that youth are aware of future roles and the significance of decisions involving content issues; able to sort content alternatives by priority, giving less significance to matters of temporary importance; and prepared to heed the pressures of parents and peers when these pressures are realistic.

AUTONOMY. The development of social competence within the family has often been discussed as the adolescent's bid for autonomy, a condition that may be considered as an aspect of competence. Mussen, Conger, and Kagan, discussing motives essential to a child's personality development, describe autonomy as "the desire to control one's actions and be free from coercive control of one's behavior by another" (1969:134). Stone and Church (1979) view autonomy as the sense of being in charge of one's own life and of being competent in making one's own decisions and carrying them through. Elder (1962) operationally defines autonomy as confidence in one's own values and independence as shown in the desire to make up one's own mind. After an extensive study, Kovar derives the following description of the autonomous process: "a temporary withdrawal from relations with others, a withdrawal (always psychological but not necessarily physical) that helps to reinforce one as a separate and distinct personality in personal relations . . . [Autonomy] is at all times either potentially or actually in the service of positive relationships" (1968:3). Rothchild suggests that, applied to behavior, "autonomy connotes sufficient psychologic separation from others so one can assume responsibility for the self and can choose and initiate action in accord with one's own independent set of guidelines" (1979:275). The autonomous individual realizes an "autonomy of values and commitments [which] implies concern for what one wants to be and stand for, a capacity to question conventional beliefs, and a willingness to act on one's own values" (p. 287).

An aspect of autonomy that is of particular interest here is moral autonomy. Psychoanalytic theory holds that moral autonomy develops during adolescence as young people internalize the values and standards of their parents. Social learning theorists maintain that, through rewards and punishments and through modeling, people can acquire moral autonomy as they acquire any social behavior. Cognitive theorists, such as Piaget and Kohlberg, argue that people progress through stages toward a reciprocal or autonomous morality, which includes an understanding of social rules as well as an appreciation of reciprocity in human relationships.

Although they outline its development differently, these three theoretical positions agree that moral autonomy is attained during the adolescent years. One who is morally autonomous relies less on external controls than on internal direction of moral judgment and behavior. It should be noted, however, that most research into moral development has investigated moral judgments and attitudes, not moral decision making in real social behavioral contexts. There is no empirical evidence for when and how judgment becomes consistently predictive of behavior. As Lewis (1981) points out, we do not know the relationship between judgment and decision making in many areas of adolescent development; future research must address this problem.

Although definitions from dictionaries, from empirical research, and from theoretical discussion do not mesh perfectly, we can say that autonomous individuals, far from shutting themselves off from others, engage in active, personal, interdependent relationships while at the same time maintaining their own distinct personalities.

The development of autonomy is a long-term process, but during the adolescent years there is a societal focus on the individual's bid for autonomy with an implied expectation that autonomy is attained at that time. But is there a certain age at which a person attains sufficient autonomy to direct his or her life, making decisions that are essentially his own? Research evidence suggests that, although age is important, there are wide individual variations in attitudes and behavior.

The development of autonomy demands give-and-take on the part of both parents and children and thus can lead to conflict, especially during a child's early adolescence when the autonomy issue is salient. The questions here are: How much autonomy is needed and wanted? How much is allowed? Adolescents may be unwilling or unable to develop full autonomy because of the economic, legal, and emotional ties that bind them to parents and because personal and social ties make them sensitive to peer pressure (Goodman 1969). Kagan holds that "the adolescent knows he must make his own decisions, but must feel free enough to ask adults for advice" (1972:98). Miller (1975) agrees that the young adolescent needs at times to stand alone, but also needs to know that there is nearby someone to turn to. Manaster (1977) posits that conflict exists within the adolescent between being fully autonomous and being able to rely on parental protection.

Developing autonomy is a problem, not only for adolescents but also for their parents, who are also facing an authority crisis (Rice 1975). For many parents the major problem is how much independence to allow an adolescent. Parents may recall their experiences with the child when he/she was younger, and have difficulty recognizing the child's present capability. The self-role definition of the child and the parent's interpretation of the child's role must undergo constant modification (Bell 1966). (Bell emphasizes the symbolic significance of a parent's recognition that a child has reached an age when something as "adult" as sexual behavior, for example, becomes relevant.) Manaster (1977), among others, notes that when conflicts occur they often pertain to the *degree* of autonomy the adolescent will be granted. Such conflicts are usually resolved informally by parent and adolescent, but occasionally require the formal intervention of a third party.

COMMUNICATION. Because the development of autonomy involves give-and-take between parents and children, communication must take place. Miller (1974) indicates that family interaction patterns exert an important influence on an individual family member's behavior. As important as family communication is, however, it is a difficult area to study objectively and at present there is very little research on this aspect of adolescent behavior and development.

While research evidence is sparse, some results are emerging that offer insights into parent-youth communication. Wollfil (1977), examining the communication patterns of children and adolescents concerning political topics, found that for sixth-, ninth-, and twelfth-graders the major sources of information were immediate family members and peers and that the information-seeking behavior of the respondents was successful. The family is a major source of information. Yet one of the most frequent complaints of adolescents is that their parents do not listen to their ideas, do not accept their opinions as relevant, and do not try to understand their feelings and points of view (Rice 1975). Adolescents want their parents to be willing to communicate. Time is often an enemy;

Satir (1972) reports that an average family spends as little as ten minutes a week together in a setting that would encourage conversation. Assumptions that family members make about each other influence communication within families; if assumptions are rigid, they can restrict the flow of information and reinforce counterproductive behavioral patterns (Boyd et al. 1974).

That communication between adolescents and their parents is difficult is almost a given, but research needs to specify reasons for the difficulty. Dubbe (1965) contends that while all young people have difficulty communicating with their parents at some time about something, more topics give difficulty with the opposite-sex parent, more topics are troublesome for boys than for girls, nagging is a major source of difficulty in communication with the opposite-sex parent, and the desire for self-reliance appears earlier among and is more important for boys than girls. Most difficulties in communicating with parents occur when the topic is sex or romance.

Most studies of parental-youth communication conclude there is a problem. Not all is bleak, however; Rothschild (cited in Lambert et al. 1972) suggests that the communication gap is not inevitable; a questionnaire survey of 1,219 high-school students showed that 38 percent considered they had good or excellent communication with their parents, 44 percent fair communication, and only 18 percent poor or unsatisfactory communication.

Present research offers evidence that is at times contradictory, but there are a few tentative conclusions one can draw from the general studies on parent-youth communication. Adolescents, through age 14, will communicate reasonably well with their parents if they have a nurturing home environment. Girls seem more willing than boys to share personal information with their parents, especially their mothers. There is a decrease in parent-youth communication during the middle years of adolescence. At times the most difficult topics for young people to discuss with parents are those related to their sexuality. Parent-youth communication is best at any stage of adolescence when there is mutual respect for opinions and concerns.

We have said repeatedly that the research literature on the development of adolescent competence is sparse. That is why we have discussed tangential areas—parental influence, autonomy, and parent-youth communication. If there is a common theme running through these diverse studies, it is that the development of competence and related qualities is quite dependent on adolescents' family relationships. An atmosphere of mutual respect and warmth which encourages the belief that one is responsible for and in control of one's life seems ideal for the growth of competence.

The research does, we think, support our general conclusion that by middle adolescence the potential for competent decision making is available; the realization of that potential depends on the social environment, of which the most significant aspect is the family. But how can this information be related to policymakers' needs?

The criterion currently used by our legal system to determine adulthood is the attainment of an arbitrarily chosen age, typically age 18. The legal system determines that some minors are mature because they live apart from their parents and are financially independent. These criteria are objective and are simple to apply. Is the adolescent 18 years old? If not, has the adolescent moved out of the parental home, and is the adolescent financially independent? Is he or she married? In such circumstances, the minor is presumed to be mature and is treated at law as an adult.

But though they are objective, these criteria are irrelevent to deciding whether a particular adolescent is competent to make certain decisions without parental control or guidance. If only these objective criteria are used, many youngsters will be incorrectly judged to be competent when they are not, or incompetent when they are competent.

Are there alternatives? Criteria for judging maturity of individual adolescents based on the kind of research done in the social sciences would create more problems than they would solve. We cannot expect judges or policymakers to test a 14-year-old for level of self-esteem, to inquire into the degree of autonomy of a 15-year-old, or to assess a 16-year-old's competence in a variety of contexts before making judgments about their maturity. The power to make such judgments would be enormous and the judgments often subjective and capricious. The present system, which uses objective criteria, makes better sense despite its inaccuracies.

The major problem with the present system is its presumption of childhood *until* age 18, and its sudden conferring of adulthood *at* age 18. Perhaps an intermediate legal status is called for, in which certain "adult" actions could be taken and decisions made independently while others would still require parental consent (see Foster and Freed 1972). Research evidence suggests that adolescents who are younger than 18 can act competently in certain areas. The challenge for social and psychological research is to determine the age at which adolescents generally can act competently in the particular area at issue (see Catton 1979; Grisso 1981). We shall have more to say about this matter in our final chapter, on social policy.

6

Sex, Contraception, and Abortion

To what extent do adolescents engage in premarital sexual intercourse? Do they use contraceptives, or rely on abortion? Do they consult their parents for information and guidance about sexuality, contraception, and abortion? These questions are important to policymakers concerned with the sexual rights of minors.

We intend to provide information about adolescent behavior for those who formulate and implement policies. Knowing what teenagers actually do is helpful in evaluating current policies and in proposing changes. If, for example, almost all minor women voluntarily inform their parents about visits to family planning or abortion clinics, laws requiring parental notification would be unnecessary.

Before assessing the reasonableness and adequacy of current social policies, let us briefly recapitulate them. In many states, it is illegal for unmarried minors to engage in sexual intercourse because all sexual intercourse between unmarried partners is illegal. Such laws impinge upon minors in particular only because minors below a certain age (the age varying from state to state) require parental consent to marry, and it is only in marriage that sexual intercourse is legal. Statutes prohibiting premarital sexual intercourse are, however, rarely enforced. Most states also have laws which presume that minors under a certain age are incapable of consenting to sexual intercourse, and that sex with an unconsenting person constitutes the crime of rape.

Although state statutes are generally silent on minors' access to contraceptive medical services, most states have adopted policies that explicitly permit minors to obtain contraceptive services on their own consent (see Chamie et al. 1982). There is also a consensus that decisions of the U.S. Supreme Court on closely related issues effectively protect minors' access to contraceptive services. For example, *Carey vs. Population Services International* (1977) held that states could not prohibit the sale or distribution of non-prescription contraceptives to minors; *Doe vs. Irwin* (1980) held that the distribution of contraceptives by public clinics, without notifying parents, did not violate parents' constitutional rights. Many private physicians and some family planning agencies, however, will not provide medical contraceptive services to minors (especially those under 16 years of age) without the consent of the parents (Torres, Forrest, and Eisman 1980).

The legal situation regarding abortion is less clear. U.S. Supreme Court decisions prevent states from requiring parental consent to abortion for all minors who wish abortions; it is unlikely that the Court would accept a state statute requiring even the notification of the minor's parents in all instances of abortion (Paul and Pilpel 1979). But the Court has affirmed a state law requiring parental notification in a case involving an immature and unemancipated minor, at least where there is no concrete evidence that parental notification would be contrary to the minor's best interest. It remains to be seen whether states can place other kinds of limits on minors' access to abortions.

The direction of policy, thus far, is toward granting minors many of the rights of adults in the reproductive health area, while recognizing the special situation of minors. But policies are still being worked out; there will be many more legislative and judicial decisions on minors' rights before their approximation to, or divergence from, adult rights is fixed.

Do adolescents follow current social norms? Are they well served by current policies and programs? What about adolescents' behavior in the areas of sexual intercourse, contraception, unwanted pregnancy, and abortion? In these areas what do adolescents do? How do they decide what to do? How much do they know? Do they tell their parents about their behavior and decisions? If they make decisions competently—based on good informaton about sexuality and reproduction, a reasoned consideration of alternatives, a system of values, and appropriate consultation with others—we can conclude that there is no need to tinker with current policies and programs. If they do not make decisions competently, we will need to explore whether the problem stems from current policies and programs, and whether alternative policies or programs might be helpful. In addition, since parents usually have the primary influence in the development of their children's competence, values, and behavior, we will also need to evaluate parents' practices in socializing and communicating with their children.

SEXUAL INTERCOURSE

Minors do not need the consent of their parents to engage in sexual intercourse, except indirectly through the requirement of parental consent for marriage. Many of the minors who engage in premarital sexual intercourse do so in their homes, and occasionally this involves the tacit consent of their parents (cf. Rodman 1971:114–116). Frequently, however, it indicates no more than that the parents are away from the home, so that the minors have the opportunity and privacy for sexual intercourse at home or at their partner's home. Of never-married women between 15 and 19 who have engaged in sexual intercourse, 23 percent report that their most recent act of sexual intercourse took place in their own home, and 51 percent that it took place in their partner's home (Zelnik and Kantner 1977). For adults, sexual intercourse has become largely a matter of mutual consent, since the remaining state laws against fornication are rarely enforced. The same is generally true for minors, though the state sometimes intervenes in cases where one partner is a minor and the other an adult. The average age of first sexual intercourse is 16.2 for young women and 15.7 for young men (Zelnik and Shah 1983).

To what extent do minors engage in premarital sexual intercourse? In 1974 an estimated 11 million 15- to 19-year-olds had engaged in sexual intercourse; in 1978, approximately 12 million (AGI 1976, 1981). A 1976 national probability sample indicated that 35 percent of never-married women aged 15 to 19 had engaged in sexual intercourse. Since we are interested in minors we will concentrate on those who were under 18 in the 1976 study. Of those aged 15, 18 percent had experienced sexual intercourse; of those aged 16, 25 percent; of those aged 17, 41 percent (Zelnik and Kantner 1977). There is evidence that such rates have been

TABLE 6.1

Percentage of Metropolitan-Area Never-Married Women with Premarital Sexual Experience, for 1971, 1976, and 1979

Age	1971	1976	1979
15	14.4	18.6	22.5
16	20.9	28.9	37.8
17	26.1	42.9	48.5

SOURCE: Zelnik and Kantner (1980)

rising since about 1967 (Chilman 1978:113–117). If we focus on national samples of never-married metropolitan-area teenagers, we can see sizable changes from 1971 to 1979 (table 6.1). For example, the percentage of 17-year-old women who have experienced sexual intercourse rises from 26 percent in 1971 to 43 percent in 1976 to 49 percent in 1979. Although the percentages for teenagers from metropolitan areas are higher than those for teenagers from nonmetropolitan areas, the percentages for both groups are rising. In another estimate of sexual activity, for 1978, Zelnik, Kantner, and Ford (1981) report the following percentages for unmarried females (and males): age 13, 2 (12); age 14, 11 (24); age 15, 20 (35); age 16, 32 (45); and age 17, 45 (56).

What is the frequency of intercourse by sexually experienced women aged 15 to 17? In the 1976 study, 20 percent of those who had engaged in sexual intercourse reported only one such experience. In the four weeks prior to their interviews, 51 percent reported no sexual intercourse, 30 percent reported one or two sexual experiences, 10 percent reported three to five sexual experiences, and 9 percent reported six or more experiences. Further, since beginning their sexually active lives, 54 percent had confined themselves to one partner, 32 percent had had two or three, and 14 percent four or more (Zelnik and Kantner 1977).

Whether we react to such information about the sexual activities of female minors with alarm or aplomb, it is clear that a sizable and growing number are at risk of becoming pregnant. Are they aware of the nature of that risk? Do they know when during the menstrual cycle they are at greatest risk? As Zelnik points out, "Knowledge of the period of greatest risk is an important topic. A major reason given by sexually active teenagers for nonuse of contraception is that intercourse took place at a time of the month when they thought they could not become pregnant" (1979:356). Zelnik and Kantner (1977) asked women when, during the menstrual cycle, they were at greatest risk of pregnancy. The percentages who correctly reported that this period is about two weeks after menstruation begins were quite low (table 6.2). Less than half of the white and the black adolescents in each age group (see "total" columns in table 6.2) answered correctly. White minors were more knowledgeable than blacks. Whites were also more likely to answer correctly with increased age and experience, while blacks were not.

In a study by Fox (1979) carried out in Detroit, both mothers and their daughters (aged 14 to 16) were asked several questions about pregnancy risk. The sample consisted of 449 mother-daughter pairs, 44 percent white and 56 percent black. One true-false question was: "A woman is most likely to get pregnant about two weeks after her period begins." Only 16 percent of the daughters gave the correct answer, in contrast to 41 percent of the mothers. (For daughters, this was the question that produced the lowest percentage of correct answers.) To the true-false question, "A girl cannot get pregnant if she doesn't come to climax (have an orgasm) during sexual intercourse," 50 percent of the daughters and 93 percent of the mothers answered correctly. Similar data are reported for six additional questions about pregnancy risk, as well as

TABLE 6.2

Percentage of Never-Married Women with Correct Knowledge of Pregnancy Risk, 1976

	All			White			Black		
Age	Total	Sexually Experienced	Not Sexually Experienced	Total	Sexually Experienced	Not Sexually Experienced	Total	Sexually Experienced	Not Sexually Experienced
15	29.5	33.5	28.6	30.5	40.5	28.9	22.7	17.6	25.9
16	33.5	42.8	30.3	39.8	50.8	36.6	18.0	17.4	18.8
17	47.0	51.7	43.7	48.0	51.0	46.2	26.6	28.4	22.7

SOURCE: Zelnik and Kantner (1977:58).

for other questions on sexual knowledge. Fox's overall conclusion was that "most daughters do not know enough about male and female sexuality, pregnancy risk, or contraception to be able to handle their own sexual standards safely, that is, in a pregnancy-free way" (1979:59).

What factors determine whether adolescent girls engage in premarital sexual intercourse? Clearly, as the Zelnik and Kantner study shows, age is one: older girls are likelier to have had sexual intercourse than younger girls. In addition, as several studies show, blacks are likelier to have had sexual intercourse than whites. Among those who are sexually active, however, whites engage in sexual intercourse more frequently than blacks (Zelnik, Kantner, and Ford 1981). Sexual intercourse is also likelier to occur "for those who date frequently, who go steady, or who consider themselves in love" (Chilman 1978:123). Finally, those daughters who have better communication and more affectionate ties with their mothers are more likely to postpone sexual intercourse (Inazu and Fox 1980; Walters and Walters 1980).

USE OF CONTRACEPTIVES

Over the past two decades it has become easier for minors, as for adults, to gain access to both nonprescription and prescription contraceptives. The situation for minors, however, is somewhat precarious. Only a few state legislatures have tried to enact a statute requiring parental consent in order for minors to have access to contraceptive medical services. Common law, however, requires parental consent for medical treatment of minors (with exceptions for emergencies and for emancipated or mature minors) and "physicians often hesitate to serve young people without first obtaining parental consent because they fear possible civil liability" (Paul 1977:4). Yet we know of no case of a lawsuit being won against a physician who provided contraceptive services to a minor (Paul and Scofield 1979).

Unlike physicians and other health-care providers in private practice, family planning clinic practitioners have much experience in serving minors and, consequently, with their needs and legal rights. As a result, family planning clinics provide excellent access to teenagers. In a survey of 1,676 family planning agencies, Torres et al. report that a very large majority serve minors without requiring parental consent. Twenty percent of the agencies have parental consent or notification requirements for patients 15 and younger; only 10 percent have such requirements for 16- and 17-year-olds. The requirements are, however, frequently waived at the discretion of a physician or for a variety of other reasons (Torres et al. 1980). It should be noted that many clinics encourage minors to consult with their parents, although they do not make it mandatory. Adolescents themselves list confidentiality ("it doesn't tell their parents") as the most important reason for selecting a family planning clinic (Zabin and Clark 1983:26).

Do minors who are sexually active make use of contraceptives? Surveys conducted by faculty members of Johns Hopkins University give detailed answers to this question. In 1976 and 1979 Zelnik and Kantner (1980) collected information by means of which they were able to divide all sexually active women (aged 15 to 19) in their samples into three groups: those who *always* used contraceptives, those who *sometimes* did, and those who *never* did. The percentage in the *always* group rose from 29 in 1976 to 34 in 1979, in the *sometimes* group from 36 to 39. The 1976 survey found that 38 percent, the 1979 survey that 49 percent, practiced contraception at their first experience with sexual intercourse. These figures indicate some improvement in the consistency of contraceptive use between 1976 and 1979.

The contraceptive methods used by women aged 15 to 19, in 1971, 1976, and 1979, are shown in table 6.3. Although the samples and the data provided are not fully comparable, as indicated in the tablenotes, we can nevertheless get an approximate idea of the changes that have occurred. Use of the pill increased sharply from 1971 to 1976 and then declined, probably because of publicity about the dangers of oral contraceptives (Jones, Beniger, and Westoff 1980). Use of the condom declined from 1971 to 1976, and then increased very slightly. Use of the withdrawal method dropped sharply from 1971 to 1976, and then increased somewhat. In summary, major changes took place from 1971 to 1976, relatively minor changes from 1976 to 1979.

TABLE 6.3

Contraceptive Method Used Most Recently by Women Aged 15 to 19: Percentages

	1971 [a]	1976 [a]	1976 [b]	1979 [b]
Pill	23.8	47.3	47.8	40.6
IUD	1.5	3.4	3.2	2.0
Diaphragm	x	x	0.9	3.5
Condom	32.1	20.9	22.9	23.3
Foam	x	x	3.8	3.9
Douche	5.8	3.5	2.8	2.1
Withdrawal	30.7	16.9	14.6	18.8
Rhythm	x	x	3.8	5.8
Other	6.1	8.0	0.2	—
Total	100.0	100.0	100.0	100.0

[a] Never-married women (includes metropolitan and nonmetropolitan areas).
[b] Metropolitan-area women (includes ever-married and never-married).
x Breakdown not given.
SOURCE: Zelnik and Kantner (1977); Zelnik and Kantner (1980).

Another source of information on contraceptive use by minors and young adult women is a study carried out by Harriet B. Presser (1974). She interviewed 408 women in New York City, aged 15 to 29, who had had a first child between 1970 and 1972. She restricted the sample to women who were born in the mainland United States, who were either white or black, and whose first children were living with them. Presser reports that 56 percent of her sample had an unplanned first birth; for those aged 15 to 19 years at the time of birth, 81 percent of the births were unplanned, for those 20 to 23, 56 percent, and for those aged 24 to 29, 30 percent. Both married and unmarried women were included in the sample, and the percentage differences in unplanned births by age are due in part to lower percentages of married women in the younger age groups.

Not surprisingly, Presser's data show that contraceptive use was related to age at first birth. She reports that "55 percent of women who had their first births at ages 15-19 had never used any contraceptive method prior to birth. This contrasts with 32 percent for those aged 20-23, and 13 percent for those aged 24-29" (Presser 1974:10).

Presser asked her respondents why they did not use contraceptives before becoming pregnant. Leaving aside those who sought to become pregnant, several reasons were reported: lack of knowledge, lack of access to contraceptives, lack of motivation, and interpersonal barriers. For example, 29 percent of the women displayed a lack of knowledge—16 percent thought they could not become pregnant at that time of the month and 13 percent thought that frequent intercourse was necessary to become pregnant. In a separate question, Presser asked respondents during which part of the menstrual period they were most likely to become pregnant. A correct answer was given by 19 percent of those aged 15 to 19, 45 percent of those aged 20 to 23, and 63 percent of those aged 24 to 29. This reveals a pronounced lack of knowledge, especially for the younger women. Assuming that some of the correct answers reflected good guesses rather than knowledge, Presser (1977) asked the women the same question one year later. Only 10 percent of the women under age 21 answered correctly both times.

Zelnik and Kantner, in their 1976 national survey, also obtained information on why young women did not use contraceptives. They were asked to select one reason, from among the reasons listed on a card, to explain their last instance of nonuse. Among women aged 15 to 19, who had experienced premarital intercourse more than once, 20 percent reported that they "didn't expect to have intercourse"; 23 percent reported that they "had intercourse at [a] time of month when [they] couldn't become pregnant." An additional 28 percent selected a variety of other reasons to explain why they thought they couldn't become pregnant—they were "too young to become pregnant" or they "had intercourse too infrequently to become pregnant" (1979:292).

Lack of motivation to avoid pregnancy (or unconscious motivation to have a baby) has often been suggested as a factor contributing to teenagers' failure to use contraceptives, but we still have only very limited information in this area (cf. Furstenberg 1976; Freeman and Rickels 1979; Rosen 1982). From 1945 to 1965 the prevailing clinical myth that substituted for knowledge held that unmarried women who became pregnant unconsciously desired pregnancy, and that for young women it served as a means of protest against adult authority. A classic book on this thesis is Leontine Young's (1954) *Out of Wedlock*. The myth could not be refuted by evidence, since women who insisted that they did not want to become pregnant were said to be unaware of their unconscious desires. The myth went hand-in-glove with state policies that severely limited access to contraceptives, especially to unmarried minors. After all, if sexually active teenagers unconsciously want to become pregnant, access to contraceptives is a moot point. Regardless of the availability of contraceptives, their unconscious desires will lead them to pregnancy. Moreover, from the moral viewpoint of the time, it was reasonable to present unmarried women with a clear choice: abstinence, or sexual activity followed by deserved punishment (pregnancy).

Even the limited information now available on reasons for contraceptive use or nonuse by teenagers indicates how provincial and shortsighted the clinical myth was. Presser (1974) reports that one of the reasons the women in her sample did not use contraceptives, even though they were not *trying* to become pregnant, was that they did not *mind* becoming pregnant. The 39 percent of her sample who gave this reason probably includes women who might be identified by a clinician as "unconsciously" desiring pregnancy. But it also includes women who, according to Luker (1975), are willing to risk pregnancy for a variety of reasons that could be considered rational. For example, they may see pregnancy as a test of their partner's commitment and they know that abortion is available. Other studies have pointed out that some women are too embarrassed to obtain contraceptives (Herold 1981) or are afraid to use the pill because of possible side effects on their health (DeLamater and MacCorquodale 1979).

Chilman (1978, 1980) and Freeman and Rickels (1979) review several studies of the psychological and motivational factors involved in the use or nonuse of contraceptives. The evidence generally suggests that these factors only partially explain contraceptive use (cf. Oskamp and Mindick 1983). Social factors such as social class, religious commitment, and the sexual attitudes of friends also affect contraceptive choices. Finally, from a policy perspective, the availability, efficacy, and safety of contraceptives are important considerations. Before the early 1970s, when effective contraceptives first became readily available to minors, the most commonly reported contraceptive techniques were use of condoms and withdrawal (see table 6.3). These were primarily under the control of men, who were less motivated to use contraceptives (Finkel and Finkel 1978), and who were culturally conditioned to equate contraception with diminished pleasure. Use of condoms and withdrawal are also methods that involve precautionary activity with each act of intercourse. When effective and intercourse independent methods under women's control, such as the pill and the IUD, became more readily available in the 1970s, many women—including teenagers—were quick to take advantage of them. This suggests that attributing deficient motivation to women was incorrect, and that the deficiencies were primarily in contraceptive technology and the system of distribution.

But we must not allow the pendulum to swing from the clinical myth of unconscious desire to a new myth of deficient technology and insufficient access (see Zelnik, Kantner, and Ford 1981). Among the reasons given for some women's—especially teenage women's—not using contraceptives is one that has to do with self-image, not with access. It is the belief that being contraceptively ready implies that one expects to be sexually active. This threatens the self-image of women who hold conservative sexual values. By not using the pill, by not wearing an intrauterine contraceptive device, by not having a fitted diaphragm and spermicide, a teenager preserves her "good girl" image. Sexual intercourse, if it does occur, is then a spontaneous and unpredictable act. Since she did not expect it, she is not contraceptively prepared for it (and vice versa). As a result she maintains her self-image as a "good girl" but risks an unwanted pregnancy, a new threat to her image (Rains 1971; Shah, Zelnik, and Kantner 1975; Fox 1977; MacIntyre 1977; Reisman 1980). As Reiss puts it, "acceptance of oneself as a sexual being with the right to sexual choice is one crucial determinant" of contraceptive use (1980:197).

Since we are ultimately concerned with whether state policy should require parents' involvement in their minor children's decisions, we shall examine the extent of consultation and discussion about contraception that voluntarily takes place between parents and children (see Furstenberg et al. 1982). Several studies suggest that the extent is considerable. Fox and Inazu (1980b) separately interviewed mothers and daughters on their communications about sex, and on most issues the aggregate figures are very similar: 75 percent of the mothers and 70 percent of the daughters reported that they had talked about birth control at least once; 30 percent of the mothers and 33 percent of the daughters reported talking about birth control five or more times in the last six months. Both mothers and daughters reported a median age for daughters of 14 as the time birth control was first discussed, and 57 percent of each group reported that it was the mother who usually initiated the discussion. The largest difference is in how comfortable they felt in discussing the topic: 76 percent of the mothers felt "very comfortable" in contrast to 38 percent of the daughters. But the significance of this difference is somewhat lessened by the 20 percent of mothers and 49 percent of daughters who were "fairly comfortable."

In a study by Torres et al. (1980) information was gathered from 1,241 unmarried minors receiving contraceptives at 53 family planning clinics throughout the United States. They were asked whether their parents knew they were visiting the clinics: 54 percent reported that their parents knew, 41 percent that their parents did not know, and 5 percent were uncertain. Those teenagers who reported that their parents knew were asked how their parents found out: 56 percent said they had told their parents voluntarily, 39 percent that their parents suggested the visit, 4 percent that their parents found out from relatives or friends, and 2 percent that the clinic required them to inform their parents. The percentage of parents who knew their minor daughters were attending family planning clinics, 54 percent, is very similar to that reported in an earlier study by Torres (1978), 55 percent. In the earlier study, 65 percent of parents of girls under age 15 knew, 59 percent of parents of girls at age 15, 58 percent of parents of girls at age 16, and 50 percent of parents of girls at age 17.

How does a policymaker facing a decision on requiring parental consent or notification react to such figures? In a majority of cases the parents are informed. Does this mean that voluntary communication between parent and child is working well and requirements would be unnecessary and intrusive? Yet many parents are not informed. Does this mean that voluntary communication is not working well and requirements are needed to inform parents and protect minors? We shall have more to say in the following chapter about the difficult decisions that policymakers must make.

What difference do birth control discussions with parents make in the sexual and contraceptive behavior of adolescent girls? Furstenberg (1976) reports that 52 percent of daughters whose mothers discussed birth control with them used contraceptives at some time, in contrast to 23 percent of daughters with whom the topic was not discussed. (The contrast is between groups in which both mother and daughter agree on whether birth control has been discussed.) Fox and Inazu (1980a), having studied 449 girls (aged 14 to 16) from Detroit public schools, indicate that the more frequently daughters have discussed sexual intercourse and birth control with their mothers, the more likely they are to reply to questions in a way that signifies knowledge about and capacity to employ contraceptives. Daughters whose mothers have discussed birth control with them by age 11 or 12 postpone sexual intercourse longer than daughters whose mothers have not discussed the topic. Fox and Inazu (1980a:26) suggest "that mothers can play at least two roles in communicating about sexuality with their daughters—the roles of protector and [of] guide." Initially, as protectors, mothers provide information on such topics as menstruation, conception, dating, and morality. Subsequently, as guides, some mothers are able to anticipate or respond to their daughters' sexual activity, and to discuss intercourse and birth control with them. The research evidence suggests that such discussions have a deterrent or delaying influence on girls' initiation of sexual intercourse and also increase the use of contraception once sexual intercourse begins. It must be emphasized, however, that these are voluntary discussions; they involve parents and adolescents who are more comfortable discussing the topics of sexuality and contraception.

UNWANTED PREGNANCY

If we are to evaluate present policies and programs addressed to minors, we must know how effective they are in preventing unwanted pregnancies. Continence would certainly prevent pregnancy, but the federal effort to encourage continence has not been in existence long enough, and has been too fragmented, to permit evaluation. Among sexually active couples, unwanted pregnancies are experienced primarily by those who never use contraceptives, do not practice contraception consistently, or use the less effective methods of contraception. The question that must be asked about policies and programs is clear enough: How successful are they in promoting consistent and effective contraceptive practices, and in thus preventing unwanted pregnancies? We have examined selected data on contraceptive use; let us now look at the incidence of unwanted pregnancy among minors.

11 Million Teenagers, published in 1976 by the Alan Guttmacher Institute, was a well-timed and well-staged presentation of the problems associated with teenage pregnancy. Its subtitle, "What Can Be Done About the Epidemic of Adolescent Pregnancies in the United States," sets a dramatic tone that is borne out by statistics like the following:

Each year, more than one million 15–19-year-olds become pregnant, one-tenth of all women in this age group. (Two-thirds of these pregnancies are conceived out of wedlock.) In addition, some 30,000 girls younger than 15 get pregnant annually. (p. 10)

In a more comprehensive follow-up report, the Institute (1981) says that in 1978, 12 million of the 29 million teenagers in the country were sexually active (7 million men and 5 million women), and adolescent pregnancies increased to 1.1 million.

The media have focused upon the problem, federal programs have until recently given increased attention to it, and social scientists are gathering information about its causes and results. Green and Poteteiger begin an article (1978) on teenage pregnancy by saying, "Teenage pregnancy has reached epidemic proportions in the United States." But there is not universal agreement about the magnitude of the problem, and there is even less agreement about how to deal with it. Some have suggested that it is being exaggerated and that organizations like Planned Parenthood and Zero Population Growth have a vested interest in sounding the alarm because the "ultimate goals of the population control lobby" involve major expansions of contraception, sterilization, and abortion services for all segments of the population (Kasun 1978:15).

Leaving aside the clash of values that underlies the debate, let us look at some of the statistics on teenage pregnancy. Zelnik and Kantner's (1980) analysis of data on metropolitan-area teenagers again provides an opportunity to examine the changes that have taken place between 1971 and 1979 (table 6.4). Among all women aged 15 to 19, including both those who did and those who did not have premarital intercourse, there is an increase in premarital pregnancy from 9 percent in 1971 to 13 percent in 1976 to 16 percent (almost one in six) in 1979. For whites the percentages rise substantially through the years, for blacks they rise slightly. The percentages for blacks are nevertheless considerably higher than are those for whites. Among those women aged 15 to 19 who had premarital intercourse, the percentages of premarital pregnancy rise very slightly from 1971 to 1976 to 1979: from approximately 28 to 30 to 33 percent (one in three). Overall, it is clear that the rise in premarital pregnancy is due, not to increases in contraceptive nonuse or failure among those who are sexually active, but to the much higher percentages of teenagers who are sexually active (see table 6.1).

The figures in table 6.4 refer to metropolitan-area women aged 15 to 19. Metropolitan-area women generally have higher rates of sexual activity and premarital pregnancy; this means that the percentages for all women aged 15 to 19 in the United States are likely to be lower, but it does not affect the upward trend. Since we are interested in minors, however, aggregate figures for women aged 15 to 19 are misleading. We therefore turn to a study in which percentages are given for each age.

What percentage of all women in a particular age have experienced a permarital pregnancy? Estimated percentages for young women between the ages of 12 and 19 are provided by Zelnik, Kim, and Kantner (1979) for 1971 and 1976. They are based on information collected from women who were between 15 and 19 years old at the time of the interview. The percentages at age 14 are very low: 0.3 in 1971 and 0.1 in 1976. The percentages by age 15 are 1.0 in 1971 and 1.5 in 1976, by age 16, 3.4 and 4.2, by age

TABLE 6.4

Percentage of Premaritally Pregnant Women Aged 15 to 19, by Race, for 1971, 1976, and 1979

Women Aged 15–19	1971			1976			1979		
	Total	White	Black	Total	White	Black	Total	White	Black
All Women	8.5	5.6	25.3	13.0	10.0	26.5	16.2	13.5	30.5
Women with premarital intercourse	28.1	21.4	47.2	30.0	26.1	40.1	32.5	29.0	45.4

SOURCE: Zelnik and Kantner (1980).

17, 7.0 and 8.5. In other words, approximately 8.5 percent of all young women interviewed in 1976 had become premaritally pregnant by age 17. The percentage of teenage women engaging in sexual intercourse has been increasing since 1976, but their effectiveness as contraceptors has not; as a result the percentages premaritally pregnant at specific ages are undoubtedly higher today than in 1976 (see Koenig and Zelnik 1982). Of course, if we were to focus only on those women who are sexually active, the percentages experiencing pregnancy would be considerably higher. For example, in 1976, the percentage by age 17 would be 25.8 rather than 8.5 percent.

A premarital pregnancy is not ipso facto an unwanted pregnancy. In 1979, for example, 18 percent of metropolitan-area teenagers who had been premaritally pregnant, and who did not "resolve" the problem through marriage, had wanted to become pregnant. In 1976, 25 percent, and in 1971, 24 percent reported that they had wanted the pregnancy (Zelnik and Kantner 1980). In 1976, among all premaritally pregnant teenagers, not just those from metropolitan areas, 23 percent said that they had wanted the pregnancy (Zelnik and Kantner 1978). Clearly, a substantial number of premarital pregnancies are wanted, for a variety of reasons (Luker 1975). Nevertheless, a very large majority of the premarital pregnancies was unwanted.

How does a teenager tell her parents about an unwanted pregnancy? A detailed study of 36 premaritally pregnant women in Aberdeen, Scotland, paints a vivid picture of the anxieties and fears they faced (24 of the 36 women were teenagers).

These fears had two consequences. One was the drama of the actual moment of telling; the other was that the parents were not told at all.

For many, telling parents was traumatic, the culmination of much anxiety. Gabrielle found she could not tell her mother face to face; instead she told her to stay upstairs and shouted the news. Tina left her mother a note when she went to work. Helen made arrangements to go to a mother and baby home, only writing to tell her parents after she arrived there. Betty used her sister as an ally . . . "My older sister was there with me and she sort of backed me up—she was standing by to help." Anne waited until several weeks after she was married. . . Several women told their parents in the presence of their boyfriends, presenting them with a package "I'm pregnant and we're going to get married" in an attempt to defuse the explosive possibilities of the first part of the statement. (MacIntyre 1977:113–114)

The parents of two women were strongly condemning, but most reacted more sympathetically than their daughters had expected. A similar finding is reported by Rains (1971): women expect much stronger moral condemnation from their parents and from others than they typically experience. As MacIntyre (1977) says, telling parents about a premarital pregnancy also means telling them that one has been sexually active, with the risk that they will define one as "a bad girl." More often, however, the women negotiated a definition of themselves as "nice girls in trouble" (which justified abortion) or as "prematurely pregnant" (in anticipation of marriage).

A minor's discussion of a premarital pregnancy with her parents is generally carried out in the context of deciding what to do about the pregnancy. Having and keeping the child is one possibility; adoption is another; abortion is a third. We have more to say about parent-adolescent communication in the following section on abortion.

ABORTION

Since the early 1900s, abortion was illegal throughout the United States, and for the most part therapeutic abortions were only available when the woman's life was threatened by the pregnancy. Between 1966 and 1972, 13 states reformed their abortion laws to permit therapeutic abortions on such grounds as preserving the woman's health, fetal deformity, and pregnancy due to rape or incest. In 1970, four states (Alaska, Hawaii, New York, and Washington) repealed their anti-abortion laws, permitting a woman to request and a physician to perform an abortion without having to rely upon limited legal grounds to justify the abortion. Although abortion remains controversial in the United States, its legal and constitutional status was strongly affected by the U.S. Supreme Court's decisions of 1973 (Sarvis and Rodman 1974). As a result of those decisions, abortion became legal throughout the United States, a woman's right to have an abortion was granted constitutional protection, and abortion became increasingly available, especially in the larger cities.

The availability of abortion to minors was not at issue in the 1973 abortion decisions (the two cases involved adults), and the Court deliberately avoided taking a position on the constitutionality of parental consent requirements. At that time, ten states required parental consent for a minor's abortion, and several states added such requirements subsequently. After 1973, the requirements were successfully challenged in most states that had such laws, and in 1976 (*Planned Parenthood of Central Missouri vs. Danforth*) and again in 1979 (*Bellotti vs. Baird*) the Supreme Court ruled that states may not arbitrarily prohibit all minors from obtaining abortions without parental consent. As a result of the liberalization of abortion statutes in about one-third of the states between 1966 and 1972, the 1973 abortion decisions, *Danforth* in 1976, and *Bellotti* in 1979, legal abortions were becoming increasingly available to minors throughout most of the 1970s.

Several obstacles to abortion also emerged in the 1970s. One obstacle, for example, is that several states enacted laws denying Medicaid funding for nontherapeutic abortions, and in 1977 the U.S. Supreme Court upheld these restrictive statutes. Second, the Hyde amendment barred the use of federal funds for virtually all abortions, including therapeutic abortions. Heatedly debated and challenged as discriminating against poor women who had to rely on Medicaid, the amendment was nevertheless passed each year beginning in 1976, and upheld by the U.S. Supreme Court in 1980 (*Harris vs. McRae*) despite a constitutional challenge. Third, groups organized to picket abortion clinics, to publicize the anti-abortion message, and to support a variety of anti-abortion bills at the local, state, and federal levels. Although many of these bills were passed, for the most part they have not passed, or if passed have been declared unconstitutional. But the zeal of the "pro-life" movement, by the late 1970s, had nevertheless offset the favorable publicity about abortion in the early 1970s (Sarvis and Rodman 1974). Fourth, the Supreme Court's decision in *H. L. vs. Matheson* (1981) upheld Utah's law requiring physicians to "[n]otify, if possible, the parents or guardian of the woman upon whom the abortion is to be performed, if she is a minor . . ." Although the decision pertains only to unemancipated minors who have made no showing of maturity (and who have not shown the abortion to be in their best interests), it nevertheless quashes the notion, encouraged by earlier decisions, that a minor's right to an abortion is virtually equivalent to an adult's, and that states could not insist on any form of parental involvement. Several states have therefore recently enacted statutes requiring parental consent or notification (Bush 1983). Finally, the Reagan administration's hostility to abortion poses a threat of unknown magnitude to its availability, especially for minors.

The annual number of induced abortions throughout the 1970s reflects the increased availability of abortion. For all women in the United States the number of reported abortions rose from approximately 193,000 in 1970 to 855,000 in 1975 to 1,239,000 in 1979; the abortion ratio (abortions per 1,000 live births) rose from 52 to 272 to 358 (CDC 1980:29). Using figures that more completely cover abortions by private physicians, the rise is from 1,034,000 in 1975 to 1,544,000 in 1980 (Henshaw et al. 1982). For minors (17 years or younger) the estimated number of legal abortions rose from 127,000 in 1973 to 167,000 in 1975 to 199,000 in 1980 (Dryfoos and Bourque-Scholl 1981:26; Henshaw and O'Reilly 1983:6).

Another perspective on the use of abortion by teenagers (aged 15 to 19) is the percentage who end a first premarital pregnancy by induced abortion. Among whites who did not marry in response to their first premarital pregnancy, and who were not pregnant at the time of the interview, 39 percent had induced abortions in 1971 and 51 percent in 1976; among blacks there was an undercount (Zelnik and Kantner 1978). Restricting the comparision on teenager abortions over time to young women (black and white) living in metropolitan areas, Zelnik and Kantner (1980) report that 23 percent had induced abortions in 1971, 33 percent in 1976 and 37 percent in 1979. The percentage of pregnancies ending in abortion was increasing, the percentage of marriages (and live births) was decreasing. By combining figures on those marrying and those adopting other resolutions, we arrive at the following distribution of responses to premarital pregnancy in 1979: marriage (typically followed by live birth), 16 percent; stillbirth or miscarriage, 12 percent; live birth without (or prior to) marriage, 42 percent; induced abortion, 31 percent.

For 1976, the percentages of young white women whose first premarital pregnancy ended in induced abortion (or miscarriage) are available by age: age 14 or younger, 29 percent; age 15, 33 percent; age 16, 39 percent; and age 17 to 19, 56 percent (Zelnik, Kantner, and Ford 1981:151).

As mentioned earlier, many minors tell their parents that they are attending family planning clinics, even though they are usually not required to do so in order to get medical contraceptive services. Do minors also consult their parents about how to deal with unwanted pregnancies; in particular, do they consult them about abortion? The question is critical, for two reasons. First, unlike other resolutions of a problem pregnancy, such as childbirth, it is relatively easy to have an abortion without one's parents' knowledge or consent. Second, this is the area pertaining to the sexual rights of minors about which there is the greatest controversy, the least consensus, and the largest number of unresolved policy issues.

There is, unfortunately, very little information about the extent to which parents are involved in abortion decisions (or, more generally, in decisions about dealing with unwanted pregnancies). One study, based on a survey of 1,170 unmarried minors who attended 52 abortion clinics across the country, reports that 55 percent of the parents of unmarried minors who sought abortions knew their daughters were doing so (Torres et al. 1980). The younger the patient, the more likely she was to tell her parents: 75 percent of minors aged 15 or less did so, 54 percent of 16-year-olds, and 46 percent of 17-year-olds. Of *all* minors, 54 percent reported that they had discussed the abortion decision with their parents, i.e., in virtually all cases where the parents knew, the decision had been discussed.

In another study, Rosen (1980) collected information from 432 minor women throughout Michigan who were unmarried and faced unwanted pregnancies. When they first thought they might be pregnant, 14 percent sought advice from their parents (in contrast to 33 percent who sought advice from their male partners and 33 percent who turned to girlfriends). When seeking pregnancy tests, 23 percent consulted their parents. After confirming their pregnancies, 57 percent consulted their parents about what to do. Confronting premarital pregnancy is a process in which the percentage of women who seek advice from their parents increases substantially at each successively more critical state. Moreover, regardless of whether they chose abortion, adoption, or keeping their children, more than 50 percent in each category reported that their mothers had had some influence on their decision.

Sensitive to the policy implications of her work, Rosen collected information on the extent and the circumstances of mothers' influence. She found that the degree of conflict daughters experienced was associated with the degree of influence their mothers had on their decisions. This suggests "that those who experienced conflict tended to turn to mothers for support or that mothers' intervention increased or produced conflict" (Rosen 1980:48). Among whites, the more competent the daughters considered themselves, the less likely they were to be influenced by their mothers. Among blacks there was no association between perceived competence and mothers' influence. Minors who made their decisions independently were more likely to perceive themselves as competent and less likely to experience conflict. Finally, a traditional or feminist orientation on the part of daughters was not associated with whether they consulted their mothers.

These findings suggest that the process of informal and voluntary communication between minor women and their parents works reasonably well, although they do not provide a direct, obvious guide to policy formulation. We shall turn to the question of policy in our Conclusion.

ATTITUDES AND VALUES

Our focus thus far has been on the sexual behavior of teenagers—intercourse, contraceptive use, unwanted pregnancy, and abortion. These are items that can be readily counted: How many teenagers have engaged in sexual intercourse? How frequently? How many have used contraceptives? How consistently? To determine the current situation in the United States, and as background for evaluating policies and programs, it is essential to provide this kind of information. But it is also essential to recognize that these behavioral items are part of a much larger system of sexuality and social relationships. What do children learn from parents and others about values and attitudes toward themselves generally and toward themselves as sexual beings? What do they learn from the informal and nonverbal behavior of their parents, as well as from their parents' explicit communications about sexual matters? What do they learn about gender roles? What do they learn about the part that sexual behavior plays within life in general? Are they learning that sexuality is a circumscribed phenomenon having to do with sexual intercourse, physical positions, and erotic techniques, or that it permeates all relationships to a greater or lesser degree? To provide a broader base from which to examine policies and programs, we shall summarize the available data on values and attitudes toward various aspects of sexuality. Not all of these data are focused on teenagers, and this represents a serious limitation. Nevertheless, since teenagers grow up within the larger society, and learn their values within the society, the information is relevant. Children are socialized by their parents, their peers, the media, teachers, ministers, and others. The values and attitudes that they learn influence their behavior and, conversely, their behavior may influence their attitudes and values.

In a probing summary of information on changes in behavior and attitudes regarding premarital sexual intercourse, Reiss suggests that "from 1880–1980 one can see an almost constant increase in the acceptance of sexuality, both within and outside of marriage" (1980:168). According to Reiss, major changes took place between 1915–1925 and between 1965–1975, with intermediate periods of consolidation. In 1963, approximately 80 percent of a representative national sample of adults believed that premarital intercourse was always wrong; in 1975 only 30 percent believed this. Reiss points to several other major changes in 1915–1925 and in 1965–1975—war (World War I and Vietnam), rising numbers of women in the labor force, and rising divorce rates. It is possible that gender role changes, including greater independence on the part of women, fueled the changes in behavior and attitudes on sexuality. Reiss' major point is that these were decades marked by social change in several areas, and that all of these changes had some influence on each other.

A national sample of teenagers (aged 13 to 18) by the Gallup Youth Survey (GYS), carried out in 1978, reported that 30 percent thought premarital sex was wrong, 59 percent thought it was not wrong, and 11 percent had no opinion. Younger teens were somewhat more conservative: among 13- to 15-year-olds, 32 percent judged premarital sex wrong and 54 percent not wrong; among 16- to 18-year-olds, 28 percent said wrong and 64 percent not wrong. Girls were more conservative than boys: 22 percent of the boys thought premarital sex was wrong, compared to 38 percent of the girls; 66 percent of the boys thought it not wrong, compared to 52 percent of the girls.

Despite an historical trend toward acceptance of a variety of forms of sexual behavior (see Clayton and Bokemier 1980), there is today certainly no unanimity on sexual standards. For example, despite the sweeping changes of the last twenty years, substantial numbers of adults and teenagers still believe that premarital sexual behavior is wrong. To portray value differences, Reiss formulated a model of four basic views of premarital sexual behavior:

1. *Abstinence:* Premarital intercourse is considered wrong for both men and women, regardless of circumstances;
2. *Double standard:* Premarital intercourse is more acceptable for men than for women;
3. *Permissiveness With Affection:* Premarital intercourse is considered right for both men and women when a stable relationship with love or strong affection is present;
4. *Permissiveness With or Without Affection:* Premarital intercourse is considered right for both men and women if they are so inclined, regardless of the amount or stability of affection present. (Reiss 1980:177)

Clearly there are adherents to each of the four standards. In focusing on change, Reiss necessarily emphasizes the extent to which adherence to abstinence (and to the double standard) has decreased while adherence to permissiveness with affection has increased. But these findings pertain to the acceptance of premarital intercourse in general; it is far from certain that adults (or teenagers) would reject abstinence and accept permissiveness to the same extent if they were considering only the behavior of teenagers.

One clue to parents' values regarding their younger children is found in a report on the American family commissioned by General Mills (1977) and based on a national probability sample of 1,230 households with children under 13. Many of the parents surveyed were trying to teach their children traditional values, even when they did not hold these values themselves. With regard to one traditional value, that "having sex outside of marriage is morally wrong," 47 percent of the parents believed it and wanted their children to believe, 25 percent had doubts but still wanted to teach it to their children, and 28 percent did not believe it and did not want to teach it to their children (General Mills 1977:82).

A study that points to relatively conservative attitudes about one's own sexual behavior is reported by Fox (1979). In her Detroit study of young women aged 14 to 16, she asked about the personal acceptability of sexual intercourse when they were in love. Only 39 percent found it acceptable, and only 10 percent of the mothers found it acceptable for their daughters.

Having young children in the family makes parents more traditional in their values, particularly in those values that they consciously want to pass on to their children (Reiss and Miller 1979). It is, however, very difficult for parents to teach values they do not believe in. Moreover, our society increasingly accepts permissiveness with affection, and this influences the attitudes and behavior of teenagers. It is not likely, from a policy perspective, that it would be feasible to promote different values for people of different ages, with minors encouraged to adopt abstinence as a value. We were not successful for long in maintaining the informal rule, "No tea or coffee until you're twenty," and sex is more stimulating than caffeine. Changes in sexual behavior in the last twenty years cannot leave anyone of conservative bent too sanguine.

The attitudes and behavior of Americans with respect to contraceptives—the birth control pill, intrauterine devices, condoms, diaphragms and spermicides—now reflect almost total acceptance by virtually all segments of the population. Reiss (1980:361) says, "the general evidence indicates that in the last two decades we have undergone a contraceptive revolution" (cf. Westoff and Ryder 1977). Despite the formal teachings of the Roman Catholic Church against the use of artificial contraceptives, the contraceptive practices of Roman Catholics in the United States are virtually identical to the practices of Protestants. On the question of whether "birth control devices should be made available to teenagers," a substantial majority of Americans is favorable, but public opinion is far from unanimous—67 percent agree, 28 percent disagree, and 5 percent have no opinion (ABC News/Washington Post 1981).

What about the attitudes and values of Americans regarding abortion? People who hold "pro-choice" views believe that women should be able to control their bodies and their decisions about childbearing, and therefore have the right to choose (or to reject) abortion. People who hold "pro-life" views object to all abortions except those undertaken to save pregnant women's lives, because they believe that abortion is the killing of an "unborn child." The United States Supreme Court, in a series of decisions since 1973, has leaned strongly in the direction of a "pro-choice" position, drawing the ire of "pro-life" partisans. As a result, we continue to see intense controversy, at the state and federal levels, about legislative and regulatory efforts by "pro-life" supporters to restrict abortions as much as possible, within the constitutional guidelines of the court. In addition, legislation and constitutional amendments that would prohibit abortions are under consideration by Congress.

Partisan views of abortion give rise to intense emotions; on the "pro-life" side they have occasionally led to violence against abortion clinics. But the sharp contrast between "pro-choice" and "pro-life" positions, while real and bitter for small groups of partisans, oversimplifies the range of values and the ambivalence (Silber 1980; Blake and Del Pinal 1981) that people feel about abortion. The National Opinion Research Center has carried out nine surveys of attitudes toward abortion between 1965 and 1980. The findings of six of the surveys are presented in table 6.5, giving the exact wording of the questions used in the surveys. The major increase in favorable attitudes toward abortion shows up between 1965 and 1972, with a further moderate increase in 1974 and a slight decrease thereafter. For example, when serious danger to a woman's

TABLE 6.5

Percentage of U.S. Adults Who Approve of Legal Abortion, 1965–1980

	1965	1972	1974	1976	1978	1980
"Please tell me whether you think it should be possible for a pregnant woman to obtain a *legal* abortion:						
(1) If the woman's health is seriously endangered by the pregnancy	73	87	92	91	91	90
(2) If she became pregnant as a result of rape	59	79	86	84	83	83
(3) If there is a strong chance of a serious defect in the baby	57	79	85	84	82	83
(4) If the family has a very low income and cannot afford any more children	22	49	55	53	47	52
(5) If she is not married and does not want to marry the man	18	43	50	50	41	48
(6) If she is married and does not want any more children	16	40	47	46	40	47

SOURCE: National Opinion Research Center surveys, as reported in Granberg and Granberg (1980). Percentages are based on respondents who answered yes or no. Respondents who gave other answers are excluded.

health is the reason, the percentages approving legal abortion rise from 73 percent in 1965 to 87 percent in 1972 to 92 percent in 1974; subsequently there is a decline to 90 percent in 1980.

It is noteworthy that the major changes in abortion attitudes and behavior occurred beween 1965 and 1975, the years singled out by Reiss (1980) as a decade of major change in attitudes and behavior on premarital sexual intercourse.

In short, the behavior and the values of Americans have been changing in tandem, and this includes the behavior and values of teenagers. The change has been toward greater acceptance of previously unacceptable forms of behavior, such as premarital sexual intercourse and abortion. Some applaud it as a movement in the direction of greater choice and freedom. Others lament it as a movement toward permissiveness, immorality, and irresponsibility. These sharply different social and moral philosophies are now very much part of the political process in the United States, and must be taken into account in evaluating and recommending social policy.

Conclusion

Policy Recommendations

POLICYMAKERS are confronted with a dilemma in dealing with the sexual rights of minors. Do they assume that youth are vulnerable and require guidance, or that youth are competent and should be granted latitude in making deicisions? The question of competence is enormously difficult. First, there are large individual variations among young people. Some are competent at 14, others not yet at 20. Second, young people vary in their level of competence from one area to another. Adolescents in general may develop competence in driving an automobile more quickly than they develop competence in making decisions about marriage. As a result it is difficult to decide when adolescents have the adult capacity to make their own decisions about contraception and abortion.

With regard to access to contraception and abortion services, laws and court decisions have created a somewhat cloudy picture. Minors in many states generally have legal access to contraception service regardless of age, although actual access varies greatly from one locale to another. A few states, however, are seeking to place some restrictions on minors' access to contraception. Regarding abortion, state legislatures differ sharply. Some are attempting to severely limit minors' rights while others are not singling minors out for special attention. Although states cannot constitutionally pass laws that require parental consent or parental notification for all minors, they may be able to require that minors who do not want to involve their parents convince a judge that they are mature enough to give informed consent or, if they are not mature, that an abortion is in their best interest (see Donovan 1981, 1982a).

The Supreme Court of the United States has been influential in bringing us to our present state of policy regarding minors' sexual and reproductive health rights. Social values, which can influence constitutional interpretations, are also extremely important. Since values about reproductive rights differ sharply and are often strongly held, our policies are not entirely clear and are subject to conflict and controversy. It therefore may be helpful to add another element to the policy debate. We have reviewed the research findings in such areas as the development of adolescent competence, trends in the sexual attitudes and behavior of teenagers, and parent-adolescent communication about sexual intercourse, contraception, and abortion. As a result, we are in a good position to assess the adequacy of current policies and to recommend new ones.

SOCIAL SCIENCE AND SOCIAL POLICY

The key question for family planning policymakers in search of empirical evidence is: When are adolescents capable of making their own decisions about contraception and abortion without parental involvement? Some related policy questions are: Are parents the best advisers for minors about family planning matters? How do minors currently make decisions about sexual behavior, contraceptive use, and unwanted pregnancies? Are adolescents (and parents) knowledgeable about family planning? Are adolescents sufficiently competent to know when to seek advice from their parents or from other adults? Do they seek such advice? What is the impact upon the family, and upon parental authority, of granting minors the right to make their own sexual decisions? What is in the best interests of adolescents, parents, and society? These are difficult questions, and they cannot be answered easily with the research findings we presently have. Nevertheless, the empirical evidence covered in the earlier chapters is helpful in beginning to answer some of the questions and making judgments about competing policy alternatives.

If we should conclude that adolescents of a given age are competent, we would then recommend policies that provide them with maximum freedom to make their own sexual decisions. If, on the contrary, we should conclude that their competence is low, we would recommend policies that provide them with protection and guidance. Another example: If we should conclude that teenagers communicate well with their parents about sexual, contraceptive, and abortion decisions, state requirements for parental involvement would be moot. If, on the contrary, we should conclude that communication is poor, we would have to confront the question of whether mandatory consent or notification requirements would be in the best interest of minors, their parents, and society. The astute reader will immediately realize that the pace of development of adolescent competence and the adequacy of parent-adolescent communication vary enormously and that policy decisions about reproductive health services are subject to the same uncertainties as are policy decisions in virtually every other area of social life.

Policy decisions about children and families are especially difficult to make, and as a result some policymakers have called for help from the social sciences. What will be the impact of extending minors' rights? Wald, an attorney speaking to social science researchers, stressed the need for cooperation between social scientists and the legal system: "Children are being given the right to request abortions, to obtain medical care, to use birth control without parental permission. We need guidance as to what are the consequences to children of different ages of having these powers" (1976:5). Ellsworth and Levy (1969–70) indicate the great difficulty faced by trial judges in child custody cases, and the need for psychological research to answer vexing policy questions. Mnookin (1978b) calls for better research information to deal with such policy issues as day care, foster care, and television advertising directed at children. It is clear that the social sciences have already made important contributions to some policy decisions (Prewitt

1980; Mosteller 1981), and that the potential exists for them to contribute to other questions—day care, child custody, and reproductive health rights.

Not all policymakers, of course, value social science research; nor are all social scientists sanguine about the contribution they can make to policy. Some believe the social sciences have virtually nothing to offer; others, more moderate in their criticism, believe the social sciences have barely begun to address policy questions and have not held policy-related research in high esteem (Coleman 1972; Scott and Shore 1979; Catton 1981). As a result, when drawing on social science data for policy purposes, we must exercise caution and recognize the limitations of the evidence (Clarke-Stewart 1977; Sharpe 1977; Scanzoni 1983). We must also exercise humility while recognizing that "humility does not necessitate paralysis" (Edelman 1973).

Relevant and unequivocal research findings do not exist for many social policy areas. Even if they are available in the academic world, they may not reach policymakers because of weak links in the chain of communication (Sundquist 1978). Further, in the heat and rush of making policy decisions, it is difficult to carefully gather and cautiously evaluate existing social science knowledge. Nevertheless, in general, it is better to formulate policy from a base of knowledge, while recognizing the limits of that knowledge. In the particular case of minors' access to abortion services, where the policy debate is taking place over a long period of time, and where major decisions are being made by the interplay of courts and legislatures, it is possible to review the empirical evidence, to use it cautiously in recommending policies, and to expect that some policymakers will pay heed to such recommendations.

THREE POLICY RECOMMENDATIONS

We have provided considerable detail in our earlier chapters in order to permit readers to make an independent assessment of whether the research evidence supports our recommendations. The research evidence we have reviewed does not lead inexorably to specific policy recommendations. As in any such endeavor, a wide gap must be bridged between research and policy. In part we have done this by carefully reflecting upon the research evidence and interpreting it in policy terms. We believe that most social scientists and policymakers will come to conclusions that are similar to our own. In part, however, we have been influenced by our values, which favor family planning and individual autonomy, tempered by a belief in children's need for guidance. Although individual freedom and choice are mainstream American democratic values, we are aware that some vocal segments of the American population are conscientiously opposed to them, at least as they are applied in the family planning area. As a result, in formulating our recommendations, we have attempted to make them politically feasible, though even so it will take political courage to promote and implement them. We also carefully elaborate our reasons for each policy recommendation.

Recommendation #1. *Legislation should be passed by the states giving minors the right to consent to reproductive health services at age 15.*

Implementation of this recommendation would make it possible for young people to obtain medical services relating to their reproductive health (including medical contraception and abortion services) at age 15 without the requirement of parental consent, parental notification, or any other type of parental involvement. They could decide for themselves whether to consult their parents or anyone else about their contraception and abortion decisions. The state would not be able to intrude, or to insist on parental intrusion.

For those under the age of 15, current policies would remain in effect. Contraceptive services would therefore remain accessible to most minors, regardless of age. For abortion services, the current uncertainties that now apply to all minors would apply only to those under 15. Some states would permit abortion services to all minors, regardless of age; other states would require parental consent or notification for minors under 15, but they would probably have to provide exceptions for those who were emancipated or mature, and an expeditious alternative for those who did not want to involve their parents and could demonstrate that the decision was in their best interest. In short, our recommendation would clarify the situation for those 15 and older. It would not bar the door to those under 15; rather it would continue to provide leeway to states in how they deal with these younger minors, and it would continue to provide leeway to younger minors in how they seek to obtain an abortion.

There is a danger that some state legislatures will try to use our data and recommendations to make parental involvement mandatory for minors under 15, while leaving the situation unchanged for those who are 15 and older. At a superficial level, our data on the greater vulnerability of younger teens can be interpreted to support that kind of change. But we disassociate ourselves from such efforts. The limited health risks of contraception or abortion and the high social and psychological risks of early childbearing suggest that minors' contraception and abortion rights should be enhanced rather than diminished (cf. Gaylin 1982). We recommend that the legal system make it possible for older adolescents to obtain all reproductive health services at their own request; for younger adolescents we are not suggesting any changes because we believe that the evidence is not strong enough to do so. If states maintain different policies for younger adolescents (or for older adolescents), it will be possible to evaluate the results and to modify policy accordingly.

Age 15 is in no sense magical, and other ages have been proposed for "adult" status regarding reproductive health services. Levy (1977) has proposed age 14 for abortion; in the United Kingdom, 16 is the age of consent for all medical services; some have proposed eliminating the age criterion altogether, making reproductive health services a basic right for people of all ages. Others do not want adulthood to begin until age 18, or even later, and have proposed eliminating the exceptions that are presently available for minors, to make access to contraceptives and abortion as difficult as possible.

Taking into account all the evidence, we think that age 15 is the most reasonable legislative choice. It can provide some protection and guidance to younger teens who have greater need for them, and for whom the danger presented by their vulnerability may exceed the danger of requiring parental (or other adult) involvement.

At the same time, it makes it easier for the large majority of teens who need reproductive health services, and who are more competent, to get these services.

We find support for our first policy recommendation in six areas, and the evidence for each area is presented below.

ADOLESCENT COMPETENCE

First, there is a growing recognition that adolescents are more competent than they are usually given credit for, and that they can demonstrate their competence if given more responsibility. As a result of this recognition, rights and responsibilities are being granted to adolescents at earlier ages. The Twenty-Sixth Amendment to the Constitution, ratified in 1971, which lowered the voting age from 21 to 18, is a prime example of the trend. In its wake many states lowered the age of majority to 18, with some reductions below 18 for a variety of other activities. Many states are also lowering the age at which adolescents may be processed by adult rather than juvenile courts. "In Vermont last spring, two boys, ages 15 and 16, allegedly raped, stabbed, and beat two twelve-year-old girls, killing one; an outraged legislature swiftly lowered the 'magic line' at which a person charged with a serious offense may be tried and sentenced as an adult. Vermont's new age limit: ten" (*Time* 1981b:80). Of course, these changes in juvenile law attribute a different kind of competence and responsibility to minors.

One of the most important U.S. Supreme Court decisions influencing the system of juvenile justice was *In re Gault* (1967). The Court decided that juveniles were entitled to due process protections, in particular the constitutional rights to legal counsel and against self-incrimination. Grisso (1981) has carried out research on whether juveniles are capable of understanding these rights, to discover whether they know what they are doing when they "voluntarily" waive these rights. He found that by ages 15 and 16 juveniles of average intelligence had a level of understanding that was not significantly different from that of adults.

In the reproductive health area particularly there have been legislative and court decisions to make contraceptive and abortion services available to many of those under age 18. Our recommendation that 15 be the age of consent for reproductive health services continues a trend that is already under way; and 15 seems reasonable in the light of current knowledge about adolescent competence and potential.

ADOLESCENT BEHAVIOR

Our policy recommendation is also supported by what we know about the sexual and contraceptive behavior of adolescents. At age 15 substantial numbers of young women are engaging in sexual intercourse, using contraceptives, and facing decisions about unwanted pregnancies. In table 6.1 we reported that 22.5 percent of 15-year-olds in a national, metropolitan-area sample have had premarital sexual experience. At age 16, the figure is 38 percent. These percentages represent large numbers of teenagers who are at risk of unwanted pregnancy and who are candidates for the use of contraceptives. According to a 1976 survey discussed in chapter 6 (Zelnik et al. 1979), a premarital pregnancy has been experienced by 0.1 percent of 14-year-olds, 1.5 percent of 15-year-olds, 4.2 percent of 16-year-olds, and 8.5 percent of 17-year-olds. These percentages were based on all women in the age groups, including those who were not sexually active. Among the sexually active, an estimated 16 percent of 15-year-olds had experienced a premarital pregnancy, 22 percent of 16-year-olds, and 26 percent of 17-year-olds (the percentage for 14-year-olds was not reported). The following estimates have been made for abortions on young women in 1980: under age 15, 15,000; ages 15–17, 183,000; ages 18–19, 261,000 (Henshaw and O'Reilly 1983). Setting 15 as the age of consent for reproductive health services would therefore include the vast majority of minors who are in need of such services.

ADOLESCENT DEVELOPMENT

The third reason for setting 15 as the age of consent for reproductive health services is that this is in alignment with what we know about the process of adolescent development. Although the research evidence reviewed in chapter 5 is conflicting—in part because different researchers have looked at different aspects of competence—there is a partial consensus that logical reasoning, in which various alternatives can be evaluated, is potentially available to the 15-year-old and, depending upon interests and experiences, can be realized in the young person's decision making in certain areas.

One could argue that differences among individuals militate against setting 15, or any other age, as the age of consent. If socialization were a mechanical process that produced uniform changes in identical products moving along an assembly line, we could pinpoint the exact moment that the product was "competent" to do its job. But the organisms differ initially because they differ genetically and, although socialization is patterned, it is also disorderly, with all kinds of chance occurrences and unpredictable interactions. We thus find infinite variety in both the process and the products. Many adults are less competent to make decisions than are some minors, and there is a great range of variation among minors in their competence. Some have argued from these premises that the "ability to make a competent decision arrives at different times for every individual" and that people are therefore best served with individualized judgments about their competence and the urgency of their problems (Fost 1976:23; Gross and Gross 1977). The difficulty with this line of argument is that it can create more problems than it solves. As Schelling has said:

Daylight saving itself is sweetly arbitrary. Why exactly one hour? . . . I know a man who has calculated that clocks should be set ahead one hour and thirty-five minutes, and another whose habits make a forty-minute shift bring the sun over the yardarm at the right moment during his August vacation. I don't think they'll ever get a bill through the legislature— for the same reason that the sprinter who can do the fastest eighty-seven yards ever stop-watched cannot get a modest adjustment accepted by the Olympic Committee. When massive social acquiescence is imperative, a one-parameter proportion will dominate the more refined proposals. (1971:62–63)

The same principle applies to setting the age of consent. Shall we refine our recommendation to 15 years, 3 months, and 6 days? Shall we eliminate age as a criterion altogether, and test each individual's competence? The first refinement is workable, but silly— since any age would be somewhat arbitrary, it simply makes sense to choose 15 or 16, and not to attempt adjustments of months or days. The second refinement is profound but unworkable. It would require a massive administrative apparatus to determine each individual's competence. How satisfied would we be with tests to determine individual competency to vote or to use contraceptives? Whom would we trust to administer the tests and to determine competence? As Mnookin says:

The fact that any age requirement will sometimes qualify older people who are quite incompetent and disqualify some younger people who are quite competent does not necessarily imply that we should allow for individual determinations of maturity or competence rather than have qualifications based on a minimum age. Qualification by individualized determinations must give some person a great deal of discretion to determine competence or maturity. But there are no litmus paper tests for judgment or maturity, and as a consequence, the power to decide this question not only can be abused but can raise profound questions concerning unequal treatment and cost. (1978b:166)

It should be noted that a decrease in the age of menarche in the United States is not necessarily a reason for lowering the age of consent. There is a dispute about the extent of decrease, but no dispute about its occurrence (Bullough 1981; Tanner 1981; Wyshak and Frisch 1982). There is also evidence that an earlier age of menarche is associated with earlier ages for sexual intercourse, marriage, and childbirth (Udry and Cliquet 1982). But the average age of menarche, about 12.5, should have only a limited bearing on the age of consent. It is the social and psychological development of adolescents, as detailed in chapter 5, and the sexual behavior of adolescents, as detailed in chapter 6, that make age 15 a reasonable choice.

JUDICIAL ADMINISTRATION

A fourth reason for our first recommendation has been implied above: it would eliminate burdensome court proceedings that often lead to delay and unequal access in obtaining abortions (Donovan 1981, 1982a). If states retain a minimum age, but lower that age to 15, the need for most individualized tests is eliminated, except for the relatively few girls under 15 who would seek exemptions from a requirement for parental involvement.

The United States Supreme Court has prohibited states from making parental consent (and perhaps also parental notification) an absolute requirement for all minors seeking an abortion. In states such as Massachusetts, Minnesota, Louisiana, and North Dakota (Donovan 1981, 1982a), that have chosen to require minors to involve their parents in the abortion decision or to seek court authorization for the abortion procedure, many teenagers are exercising their option to go to court to try to persuade the judge that they are mature and hence capable of making their own decisions, or that an abortion without parental involvement is in their best interest. Dealing with a growing number of these cases, at a time when the judiciary is already overburdened, will be necessary but troublesome (Johnson 1982). A state that follows our recommendation, however, would eliminate these burdensome administrative proceedings for the vast majority of minors and would still be able to make a judgment about whether to require parental or professional adult guidance for younger, more vulnerable teenagers.

The courts have made it clear that age will not become a suspect category, like race, or even a category subject to intermediate scrutiny (CRS 1979). Legislation that differentiates by age is therefore likely to be constitutional, as long as it serves a rational purpose. But by using 18 as the age of consent for reproductive health services, and by permitting individual exemptions, the jammed judicial process that the courts are trying to avoid by permitting "arbitrary" distinctions by age may become a reality nonetheless.

Turning these difficult decisions over to the medical profession or to agency counselors (cf. Ooms 1981) is hardly more satisfactory. Judgments of "maturity" and "best interests" are highly subjective, thus creating a potential for hypocrisy and abuse. Earlier experiences in which the medical profession was given the responsibility for making abortion judgments based on whether the pregnancy endangered the woman's physical or mental health are not encouraging. In the United States, for a period of time, some "pro-abortion" psychiatrists uneasily and arbitrarily provided access to abortions on mental health grounds (Sarvis and Rodman 1974). In Canada, since 1969, therapeutic abortion committees at hospitals have interpreted the law in vastly different and highly ideological ways (Badgley Report 1977; Rodman 1981). These judgments on "health" grounds provide easier abortion access to women who have the social and financial resources to find a physician or hospital with sympathetic values to make the desired decision. There is good reason to believe that judgments on "maturity" and "best interest" grounds would be handled in a similarly ideological and unequal manner.

By establishing 15 as the age of consent for reproductive health services, particularly for abortions, we would eliminate the need for burdensome administrative machinery and difficult (and potentially ideological and unequal) administrative decisions for the vast majority of minors.

VOLUNTARY COMMUNICATION

A fifth reason for our policy recommendation is its reliance upon voluntary communication between parents and their children who are 15 years of age or older. The alternative, to insist upon forced communication (which is what parental consent or notification amounts to) for all adolescents up to age 18, does not serve anyone's interest.

Some members of Congress have argued that a parental notification requirement in the Family Protection Act, introduced in both the Senate (S. 1378) and the House (H.R. 3955) in 1981, "protects the lifeline of communication between parents and their children in need," and generally supports the family (Washington Memo, July 17, 1981). In 1982, the proposed regulation by the Department of Health and Human Services to require parental notification for prescription contraceptives drew a storm of protest, with groups such as the Young Women's Christian Association, Family Service Association of America, and National Urban League pointing out that the regulation would lead to family conflict rather than harmony (Kenney, Forrest, and Torres 1982).

In a national survey of 375 family planning agencies, more than half (54 percent) encourage teenagers to involve their parents, but they do not require it. Moreover, 85 percent of the agencies have at least one program that directly involves parents, e.g., parent discussion groups. The data in this study suggest that parent-child communication is better among patients of family planning clinics that encourage voluntary communication than among those that require it. The authors conclude that "mandatory notification procedures do not appear to promote parental involvement. On the other hand, policies which encourage rather than require teenagers to inform their parents of their participation in family planning programs are significantly related to higher levels of parental involvement" (Furstenberg et al. 1982:144).

Several states have argued that they require parental consent for abortions in order to support parental authority and maintain family harmony. Some courts have accepted and some have rejected such arguments. The United States Supreme Court seemed to reject the argument in *Danforth,* a parental consent case (see chapter 4), and to accept it in *Matheson,* a parental notification case.

Several lines of research evidence suggest that the courts have been correct when they rejected arguments that parental consent or notification requirements promote family harmony. We know that communication between parents and adolescents tends to be better in homes where parents and children have earlier established good relationships. It is in these homes that adolescents are likelier to consult their parents about important decisions. To insist on "forced communication" regarding contraceptive or abortion services is to place a heavy burden primarily upon those adolescents who are in less harmonious families. The harmony in these families may be tenuous, and legislative requirements may shatter rather than shore up the family.

As we pointed out in chapter 6, a considerable number of unmarried minors now consult with their parents about their sexual decisions. For example, 54 percent of unmarried minors who attend family planning clinics and 55 percent of those having abortions report that their parents know what they are doing. A minor's judgment about whether to consult her parents is based on years of experience with and knowledge about them. Although not infallible, her judgment is as sound a basis as any for determining whether to involve her parents in a family planning decision. Undoubtedly many teenagers would be pleasantly surprised by the support of their parents, if they were to consult them. But many would experience rejection and punishment. Under the circumstances it seems that the best policy, at least for minors age 15 and over, is to rely upon voluntary communication between adolescents and their parents.

UNIQUENESS OF REPRODUCTIVE HEALTH DECISIONS

A sixth and final reason for our first policy recommendation is the uniqueness of reproductive health decisions. Our argument to lower the age of consent in this area is not meant to be generalized to other decision-making areas. Nor have the courts, in expanding the reproductive health rights of minors, extended their reasoning or their decisions to other areas; the courts have recognized that reproductive health decisions are uniquely urgent, important, and sensitive.

Decisions about contraception and abortion are urgent because teenagers engage in sexual activity whether or not they have access to medical contraceptives, and because an unwanted pregnancy does not slow down while decisions are made about how to resolve it. We know that many teenagers engage in sexual activity without using any form of contraception, and that 50 percent of first premarital pregnancies among teenagers occur within six months after the initiation of sexual activity (Zabin, Kantner, and Zelnik 1979). Therefore, once a sexually active teenager decides to use medically prescribed contraceptives, they should be provided as quickly as possible. Sexual intercourse and unwanted pregnancy will not wait for decisions to emerge from a process of required consultation and possible conflict with parents. Unless we are prepared to accept larger numbers of unwanted pregnancies, it does not make sense to hold a teenager's decisions about contraceptives hostage to legally required parental involvement.

The same argument applies to a decision about abortion. A minor with an unwanted pregnancy faces several options, one of which is abortion. We know that abortions are safer the earlier they are performed. It is therefore a perverse social policy that would enforce delay upon a woman who has decided on abortion, and this is even more serious for minors, who already have their abortions later than other women. Decisions for abortion must be made promptly. Any system that places obstacles in a woman's path, be they hospital abortion committees or consent requirements, contributes to delay and makes the procedure more dangerous (Rodman 1981). Although this argument applies to all women, including minors below age 15, we are arguing only for a policy that applies to older women because we acknowledge the special vulnerabilities of younger teenagers.

Decisions about contraception and abortion have important consequences for minors. An unwanted pregnancy, and particularly an unwanted birth, has a tremendous impact upon a woman's life. Teenage women are as physiologically capable of bearing healthy children as older women, except for very young teenagers. Many earlier studies incorrectly attributed poor biomedical results to teenage childbearing because they did not adequately control for several confounding factors (Phipps-Yonas 1980; Gunter and LaBarba 1981). The social, economic, and medical circumstances of childbearing minors subject them and their children to several disadvantages. Such factors as greater poverty, less adequate pre-natal care, and poorer nutritional status contribute to these disad-vantages. There is a voluminous literature on the ill effects of childbirth and child rearing upon teenagers and their children (Nye 1976; Furstenberg 1976; Baldwin 1976; Card and Wise 1978; McKenry, Walters, and Johnson 1979; Bolton 1980; McAnarney and Thiede 1981; Moore et al. 1981). Among the areas in which negative effects have been reported for minors, their children, and society are arrested educational careers, arrested social activities, limited occupational opportunities, greater health risks, and greater societal welfare costs. By providing women aged 15 and over readier access to contraception and abortion services we can re-duce the magnitude of these problems.

Contraception and abortion decisions are also sensitive deci-sions. Sexual activity, contraceptive use, and abortion are among the most sensitive and emotional topics in our society. Parents and children discuss these topics less than other sexual topics and are more discomfitted by them (Fox and Inazu 1980a, 1980b). Sub-stantial numbers of minors who currently get contraception and abortion services would not do so if they were required to inform their parents (Torres et al. 1980; cf. Herold 1981).

The uniqueness of contraception and abortion decisions—their urgency, importance, and sensitivity—is a strong argument in fa-vor of our first policy recommendation. At the same time, because these decisions are unique, anyone who fears that implementing our recommendation would lead to an extension of minors' rights in other areas can put aside that fear. Both empirical evidence and common sense indicate that reproductive health decisions are unique. The courts have begun to recognize and acknowledge that uniqueness. It is precisely because these decisions are unique that our first policy recommendation makes sense. And because they are unique our policy recommendation is also politically feasible—it would not jeopardize the legal doctrine of parental prerogative and it would leave parental authority and parental control intact in other areas.

Recommendation #2. *Policies should be adopted to encourage the development of effective, multifaceted educational programs in human sexuality that are sensitive to all value positions.*

These policies could be adopted by federal or state governments, or by private foundations: they would make funds available for developing innovative educational programs in human sexuality. Ideally, such programs would be aimed at *all* age groups and would be part of a wider program of interpersonal education that would include family life education, parent education, marital enrichment, education to cope with stress, and similar efforts. Insofar as all of these educational efforts are concerned with improved interpersonal communication and personal living, it is reasonable to expect that they can be effectively coordinated.

Since our concern here is with adolescent competence and vulnerability in the sexual area, we shall focus our discussion on programs that attempt to improve parents' and children's knowledge and communication about human sexuality. By human sexuality we do not mean sex education that confines itself to the anatomy and physiology of reproduction, to methods of contraception, and to venereal disease. Human sexuality also encompasses the social and psychological context of our identities as men and women (Roberts 1980; Laws and Schwartz 1977). From this perspective it is not sexual intercourse but sexual identity and interpersonal relationships that are the core of human sexuality.

The overall goal of such a multifaceted educational program is improved knowledge and communication for parents and children, and indeed for all members of society. At the present time hundreds of therapies and training programs flourish, or at least compete, all with the vague goal of improving interpersonal relationships. In the absence of objective information about their benefits, potential consumers have great difficulty in making intelligent choices. By challenging these therapies and training programs to develop clear goals, to delineate measurable objectives, to coordinate their services, and to evaluate results, we would serve not only parents and children, but all consumers of these services.

The educational program we are recommending would deal with the physical, social, and emotional aspects of sex, including information about conception, contraception, pregnancy, childbirth, abortion, and families. These topics can be taught in ways that respect all value positions—except for the value position which holds that they should be taught only by the family. There is widespread agreement that the family should be the primary source of education in human sexuality. For the present, however, leaving the topic to the family is similar to leaving the teaching of reading, writing, and arithmetic to the family. All of these topics are basic to survival in contemporary society, and the family cannot, or at least does not, teach them adequately.

We need to be forthright in advocating public programs of education in human sexuality. First, however, we must develop better educational programs, and better-trained teachers, so that we can be confident about the programs we advocate (Gaylin 1981). One approach is to bring together experts from different disciplines and different value persuasions to develop the educational programs. If one discipline's facts are another discipline's myths, perhaps a third discipline can separate fact from myth. Then we shall see how much information we have about human sexuality that is not merely the ideological property of one discipline or profession.

ADOLESCENT KNOWLEDGE

In addition to the general advantage of reaching consensus about our knowledge of human sexuality—and assuming that we shall reach such consensus—there are a number of specific reasons for moving ahead with our second recommendation. The first is to improve the knowledge of adolescents. At present there is considerable ignorance among teenagers, and that ignorance is costly. As we saw in chapter 6, close to half of all teenage women in the United States have engaged in sexual intercourse before the age of 18; approximately half of the women between 15 and 19 did not use contraceptives during their first experience with sexual intercourse; approximately one-fourth never used contraceptives; and fewer than half know when, during the menstrual cycle, they are at greatest risk of pregnancy. One could say, about such summary information, that there are small islands of knowledge in a vast sea of sexual ignorance. A properly planned program of education in human sexuality would be able to expand the islands and to shrink the sea.

There are substantial differences in knowledge according to age. In table 6.2 we saw that 30 percent of 15-year-old women knew when they were at greatest risk of pregnancy, in contrast to 34 percent of 16-year-olds and 47 percent of 17-year-olds. In a study by Fox (1979), also reported in chapter 6, 16 percent of 14- to 16-year-old daughters, and 41 percent of their mothers, correctly answered a question about when a woman is at greatest risk of pregnancy. Unless we believe that ignorance is bliss, we should be able to agree that it is good to know the time of greatest pregnancy risk. And in an era when sexual interests and sexual messages are pervasive, we surely can find a way of teaching that knowledge. That specific objective in itself is, of course, limited. How well would the information be understood? How well would it be integrated with other knowledge about human sexuality? Obviously we oversimplify by singling out one item of information. But it is an example of an area where we can probably achieve consensus that knowledge is better than ignorance, and where we can reasonably expect to increase knowledge with the appropriate educational programs.

PARENT-CHILD COMMUNICATION

A second reason for our second recommendation is that it would improve parent-child communication about human sexuality. There is widespread agreement among both parents and children that parents are a preferred source of sexual information (Roberts, Kline, and Gagnon 1978; General Mills 1979). Bennett and Dickinson asked a sample of 18- and 19-year-old college students, "Who do you think should have the primary responsibility for teaching young people about sexual matters?" (1980:117–120). Parents were preferred by 76 percent of the females and 50 percent of the males;

teachers were the second preferred group, listed by 13 percent of the females and 22 percent of the males.

Despite the pronounced preference for parents, however, parents are seldom identified by their children as an important source of information (Gebhard 1977; DeLamater and MacCorquodale 1979; Fox 1981). For both sons and daughters, parents are almost uniformly listed as less important sources of information than teachers, and often as less important than either peers or the media (Bennett and Dickinson 1980). On such specific items as birth control and venereal disease, parents are especially low in importance as a source of information (Bennett and Dickinson 1980). Fox and Inazu (1980b) report that mothers and daughters have greater difficulty in talking about birth control and sexual intercourse than about menstruation, dating, and sexual morality.

Since parents are a preferred source of sex information for children, it ought to be possible to develop a multifaceted educational program in human sexuality that will encourage better communication between parents and children. There is evidence that improved communication can be achieved if both parents and children are involved (Goodman and Goodman 1976). Some parents are unable to accept the developing sexuality of their children, and parents and their children are often uncomfortable about discussing certain sexual topics. A program that incorporates human sexuality education and parent education should therefore be helpful. One advantage of increasing voluntary communication about human sexuality between parents and children is that such communication is associated with delayed sexual intercourse by teenagers, and with more consistent use of contraceptives once sexual intercourse is begun (Wagner 1980).

Some caution about the relationship between family communication and effective contraceptive use is suggested by a recent study by Herceg-Baron and Furstenberg (1982). Among adolescents attending family planning clinics in Philadelphia, they found that those who could talk to a family member about sex and birth control were somewhat better contraceptors, but the differences were small and not statistically significant.

In general terms, we would expect that an established pattern

of communication is more effective than recently introduced communication, and that voluntary communication is more effective
than mandatory communication. Moreover, the nature of the communication would be of critical importance.

ADOLESCENT POTENTIAL

A third reason for developing a multifaceted educational program
in human sexuality, aimed at all age groups, is the known potential for competent decision making by early adolescents, and the
need for information in specific areas in order to develop that potential (cf. Hobbs and Robinson 1982). Since contemporary American teenagers must make many decisions about human sexuality,
it is important to provide them with sound information upon which
to decide. The educational program that we envision would provide
such information and would therefore increase the competence and
responsibility of adolescents' decision making.

One promising approach is a program that provides both information and practice at making decisions. Schinke, Blythe, and
Gilchrist provided cognitive and behavioral training to a group of
high-school sophomores: "Reproductive biology and contraceptive
methods were covered by guest speakers, audio-visual aids, and
Socratic discussions" (1981:452). Subsequently the students
learned a problem-solving sequence, and were "guided through the
sequence as they confronted decisions about dating, sexuality, birth
control, pregnancy, abortion, childbearing, and parenthood" (p.
452). Compared to a control group, those who received the training were more competent at dealing with human sexuality issues—showing more knowledge, better problem-solving abilities,
and more effective patterns of interpersonal communication; in addition, six months after the training, they were "more favorably
disposed toward family planning and were practicing more effective contraception than were control-condition adolescents" (p. 453).

Experience-based education can contribute significantly to adolescents' development. In a national study reviewing twenty-seven
school programs, comprising such activities as voluntary community service and career internships, Conrad and Hedin (1982) conclude that experience-based education can have a positive impact
upon the personal, social, and cognitive development of adoles-

cents; among other things, these programs contribute to self-dis-
cipline and responsibility.

EARLY INFORMATION

A fourth reason for the second recommendation is the serious need
for reliable information about human sexuality at an early age. Very
young teenagers are engaging in sexual intercourse, often without
using contraception, and are having unwanted pregnancies. These
younger teens tend to have little knowledge about human sexuality, and poor communication with their parents. An effective program of education in human sexuality, through the schools or the
media, could reach these teens, increase their knowledge, and perhaps improve their communication with parents. Radio and television advertising for contraceptives, if it could creatively combine
educational with commercial goals, is potentially an important vehicle for reaching all age groups, including teenagers. One cannot
expect media involvement in the near future, however, considering the results of a poll sponsored by the National Association of
Broadcasters. They report that "most Americans would find television advertisements for contraceptives distasteful and embarrass-
ing," thereby making the possibility of such advertising less likely
(Mayer 1983; see also Donovan 1982b).

Many young adolescents are little aware of the risk of pregnancy
or of the range of contraceptive possibilities until after an initial
pregnancy. More than 20 percent of all initial premarital pregnancies among teenagers occur during the first month of sexual activity; 50 percent occur during the first six months (Zabin, Kantner,
and Zelnik 1979). Several researchers have drawn attention to the
need to reach adolescents before they engage in sexual intercourse
(Zabin and Clark 1981; Baldwin 1981), or before their first pregnancy or their first child (Presser 1974). An unwanted pregnancy
or unwanted birth brings an adolescent to a professional agency
where she has the opportunity to learn about effective contraception. But having the first child has a profound impact upon a teenager, and can permanently reduce her chances for education and
employment.

One way to provide information to young teens, before they engage in sexual intercourse or become pregnant, is a strong and

effective public program of education in human sexuality. In a study of 1,341 teenaged abortion patients in a Houston hospital serving an indigent population, Dworkin and Poindexter (1980) found that 91 percent used no contraceptives or used a contraceptive method improperly. Some, for example, used birth control pills sporadically, borrowing them from friends. The investigators concluded that we need to focus attention on reducing the probability of pregnancy among teenagers through a comprehensive program of early sex education in the schools.

In their 1979 national survey, Zelnik and Kim (1982) report that approximately 75 percent of never-married women aged 15 to 19 had taken at least one course in sex education, and approximately 85 percent of these had learned about contraception in the course. One course is not a comprehensive program, and the percentages taking sex education, as reported by Zelnik and Kim, are higher than other estimates. For the adolescents surveyed, they report that taking a sex education course is not associated with sexual activity—that is, sexual intercourse took place to the same extent among those who had and those who had not taken a sex education course. Those who had taken a course, however, were more likely to have used some method of contraception at the time of first intercourse, and were less likely to have experienced a premarital pregnancy.

Research evidence suggests that comprehensive programs in human sexuality could lead to a reduced level of premarital sexual intercourse, especially among young adolescents, to more effective contraception for those who engage in sexual intercourse, and hence to a reduced rate of unwanted pregnancy.

SUCCESS OF PROGRAMS

A fifth reason for recommending educational programs in human sexuality is the evidence that such programs can be effective. In a thorough review of the impact of programs in sex education, Kirby, Alter, and Scales (1979) point out that, although the evidence is limited, it does indicate positive results. Most programs that have been evaluated have increased students' knowledge, "but they do not change the students' personal values that guide their own behavior" (Kirby et al. 1979:5). Some programs appear to have increased the use of more effective methods of contraception, decreased the use of ineffective methods, and decreased the amount of sexual intercourse without contraception.

A high school program in St. Paul, Minnesota, combining family planning services and education, dramatically decreased pregnancies. In a junior-senior high school, over a three-year period, the pregnancy rate fell by 56 percent; in two senior high schools, over a three-year period, the pregnancy rate fell by 23 percent (Edwards et al. 1980).

Sex education is included in the school curriculum in highly diverse ways. It may be a separate course, a section of a course, a single lecture or film, or integrated into other course work. As a result, it is difficult to determine how many students are exposed to sex education, and to what extent. Peter Scales (1981) cites one survey that reports 35 percent of public and private schools have a separate course in sex education; another survey reports that 40 percent of teenagers 13 to 18 years old have had a sex education course; and another survey reports that 70 percent of teenage women, aged 15 to 19, have had a sex education course. Scales (1981:559–560) also points out that most sex education focuses on "the menstrual cycle, venereal diseases, and reproductive anatomy," rather than on a comprehensive curriculum including such topics as contraception, masturbation, decision making, emotions, and personal values (see also Orr 1982; Pilpel and Rockett 1981). One study has estimated that no more than 10 percent of students take a comprehensive course in human sexuality (Kirby, Alter, and Scales 1979).

Another paper that reviews the effects of sex education on various populations—medical students, college students, educators and counselors, and teenagers—found that gains in sexual knowledge and more tolerant sexual attitudes were typical. The general review by Kilmann et al. (1981), however, covers only three studies dealing with adolescents. Their review points out that most of the literature consists of descriptive reports which stress the importance of sex education without evaluating its effectiveness. These descriptive reports were ignored by Kilmann et al. (1981), who reviewed only evaluative studies that included pre-program and post-program measures. Most of the evaluative studies had methodological flaws, such as the lack of equivalent control groups. Sex education courses, especially at the pre-college level, therefore still need to be carefully evaluated before we can speak with confidence about their impact upon students' knowledge, attitudes, or behavior.

The presently available positive results are promising enough, however, and the need is great enough, to warrant attention to developing and evaluating programs of education in human sexuality. We believe that much more can be done to coordinate the efforts of several disciplines and several training approaches, in order to develop exemplary, multifaceted educational programs. Individual disciplines and programs may have to relinquish ideological commitments in order to develop a model program that is based on sound evidence from all fields, and that respects many value positions (see Rodman 1970; Gordon 1981).

Recommendation #3. *Greater federal support should be provided to make reproductive health services available to adolescents on a voluntary basis.*

Adolescents are frequently unable to pay for reproductive health services. If they are required to involve their parents in paying for services, confidentiality is lost, and the voluntary nature of their communication with parents is also lost. It is therefore important to maintain publicly supported services for adolescents, especially since these services are highly cost effective. By increasing rather than decreasing federal support for family planning services, and by increasing the number of agencies and clinics that provide teenagers with effective and confidential services, we would make it possible for more teenagers to get responsible advice and comprehensive service in sexual health. This would, in effect, make it possible for adolescents to exercise responsibility and competence in their sexual behavior. It would almost certainly fulfill one of the goals about which there is consensus in American society—reducing the rate of unwanted pregnancy among teenagers.

Conservative scholars and policymakers have raised several fundamental questions about the policy of making family planning services readily accessible to adolescents. Does ready access lead to earlier and more frequent premarital sexual intercourse? Does it contribute to a moral climate of sexual promiscuity? Does it increase unwanted pregnancy and illegitimacy? These questions cannot be dismissed out of hand, but present evidence suggests that those who raise them are misguided—that, on the contrary, a conservative policy to reduce access to contraceptives would substantially increase unwanted pregnancies without having much impact upon premarital sexual intercourse.

UNWANTED PREGNANCY

One reason for our third recommendation has been implied above: there is a consensus that unwanted pregnancy is a problem, and there is evidence that greater access to family planning services will reduce the rate of unwanted pregnancy.

Conservative or liberal, young or old, Democrat or Republican, there is agreement in American society upon the need to reduce unwanted teenage pregnancy (Kirby, Alter, and Scales 1979). Whether individuals refer to the current state of affairs as an epidemic or as a chronic problem, whether they approach the issue from a moral or pragmatic viewpoint, virtually everyone would like to reduce the rate of unwanted pregnancy. It is a costly problem for society as well as for individual teenagers and their families.

Evidence of this consensus can be seen in the unending stream of popular materials published on the topic. Another type of evidence is the support of a majority of Americans for various measures aimed at decreasing teenage pregnancy. For example, 77 percent of a national sample approve of schools giving courses in sex education (16 percent disapprove and 7 percent have no opinion); nine out of ten of those who approve of sex education in the schools also approve of having these courses deal with birth control; and 56 percent of a national sample approve of making birth control devices available to teenagers (35 percent disapprove and 9 percent have no opinion) (GOI 1978).

There is also evidence that increased access to family planning services reduces the rate of unwanted pregnancy. A combined program of education and family planning services in several St. Paul junior and senior high schools decreased the rate of unwanted pregnancy 56 percent in one school, and 23 percent in two others (Edwards et al. 1980). Using 1970 census data, Cutright and Jaffe were able to show that access to publicly supported family planning services reduced unwanted fertility among poor women, both white and black, and among teenagers. They demonstrated that the most important variable in reducing unwanted fertility is the number of clinics and agencies providing family planning services to needy women. As a result, they concluded that the "significant program effects demonstrate a genuine need for organized family planning services even in an industrialized nation like the United States: if no need existed, there could be no program effects" (1977:119).

One study reported that during the 1970s "2.6 million unintended adolescent pregnancies were averted" by federally funded family planning programs, and that in 1979 alone an estimated 417,000 unintended pregnancies were averted (Forrest, Hermalin, and Henshaw 1981:109).

Several other studies report similar evidence. Okada and Gillespie (1977) showed that family planning clinics were highly effective in helping low-income women prevent unwanted pregnancies. Concerned about the "very high risk of pregnancy in the early months after initiation of sexual activity," Zabin demonstrates the potential impact of the early use of medically prescribed contraception in reducing unwanted pregnancy among unmarried teenagers (1981:72). Many other studies, using actual or hypothetical data, also point to the effectiveness of family planning programs in reducing unwanted pregnancy. We offer one final example. In studying a Southern city with a strong family planning program that was accessible to teenagers, and a Southern town that did not provide services to teenagers, Allen and Bender (1980) found that the city was more successful than the town in reducing unwanted fertility among teenagers. Moreover, there was general agreement in the town, by professionals and policymakers, of the need for improved family planning services. This example reflects the generally more conservative ideology in rural communities and their higher level of unmet need for family planning services (Torres 1979).

EQUITABILITY

A second reason for our third recommendation is that continued federal support is needed to assure that family planning services will be provided to minors on an equitable basis. Without direct federal support, some state and local governments will set up barriers to or will altogether abandon family planning services for teenagers. Even with federal encouragement and support, there are substantial differences from one area to another in the availability of services to teenagers, and to women generally (Alexander, Williams, and Forbush 1980). Reducing federal support for family planning services, or eliminating categorical programs that target funds to family planning services, will sharply increase these differences. This will make teenagers in certain states and counties hostage to a reigning conservative ideology that seeks to limit minors' rights in the reproductive health area. The result, we predict, will be opposite to what these conservative policymakers desire. We will wind up with more unwanted pregnancies, more abortions, and more illegitimacy. Or, if conservatives are successful in choking off legal access to abortion for teenagers, the result will be a dramatic increase in the rate of illegitimacy followed by a substantial increase in the cost of public welfare.

Because of the unquestionable need for family planning services for minors, and the clear evidence of the effectiveness of such services in reducing the rate of unwanted pregnancy, federal support should be continued and expanded. One study has estimated that organized family planning programs averted more than 2.6 million unwanted adolescent pregnancies between 1970 and 1979. Had these pregnancies not been averted, there would have been approximately 1.4 million additional abortions, 900,000 additional births, and 300,000 additional miscarriages (Forrest, Hermalin, and Henshaw 1981).

The Select Panel for the Promotion of Child Health, consisting of seventeen experts from various health and social service fields, recommended that "categorical funding for family planning services be expanded to assure that these services continue to be made available in a variety of settings, and that all persons who wish to make use of family planning services, including counseling, will have access to them" (SP 1981:270). Although not unanimous, the overwhelming weight of professional opinion supports an expanded federal role in providing contraceptive services to adolescents on a voluntary basis.

COST EFFECTIVENESS

A third reason for our recommendation is the high degree of cost effectiveness of family planning services. One study estimated that the average annual cost in 1976 of providing one patient with family planning services was $66 (Torres 1979). Another study has investigated the short-term savings to government because of family planning services delivered to low-income women between 1970 and 1975. By focusing on unintended births averted in each year, and the medical and public assistance costs that were saved in the following year, Cutright and Jaffe (1977) estimated that each $1.00 in government expenditure produced $1.80 in government savings. This is a remarkably high short-term benefit/cost ratio, and it does not attempt to calculate costs for public assistance beyond the first year, or costs due to lost work income resulting from pregnancy or childbearing, or any of the social or emotional costs associated with unintended pregnancy and childbirth.

Similar findings on the cost-effectiveness of family planning programs are reported by Chamie and Henshaw (1981). For every $1 spent by federal and state governments in 1979, approximately $2 were saved in health and welfare costs during the following year. These are savings in public expenditures that would otherwise have been paid for such items as childbirth, pediatric care, and public assistance to low-income patients. For teenagers, the public sector savings were approximately $3 for every $1 spent. Once again, the short-term financial benefits of the family planning program are substantial. Chamie and Henshaw suggest that the savings they report are conservative estimates because they ignored public sector costs that stem from lost educational and work opportunities, as well as public assistance costs that would be incurred in subsequent years.

EVALUATION

There is a general consensus in American society that unwanted pregnancy, especially among teenagers, is a serious social problem. Government policies that affect the legal status, the knowledge and attitudes, and the access of teenagers with regard to contraception and abortion are therefore of critical importance. The policies we are recommending, we believe, would do more to reduce unwanted pregnancy than current policies or other policies that have been proposed. Moreover, our recommended policies would not interfere with parental authority or family harmony; on the contrary, we believe that our policies would enhance them by encouraging voluntary family communication and by preventing disruptions brought about by forced parental involvement.

Although our recommendations are based on substantial evidence from social science research, others who are presumably reading the same research findings come to startlingly different conclusions. This is because strongly held values and beliefs about family planning enable some to blink the facts. It is therefore imperative, regardless of which policies are adopted, to evaluate them continuously and carefully in order to be able to change them when and if needed.

For best results, we believe that all three of our policies should be implemented. The first policy recommendation, to give minors the right to consent to reproductive health services at age 15, is only of limited use unless such services are readily accessible to them. Consequently, our third recommendation, to increase federal support for reproductive health services, is an important complement to the first. And our second policy recommendation, which is aimed at improved knowledge and attitudes about sexuality, would encourage improved parent-child communication and more responsible decision making by adolescents. This would lead, among other things, to better use of the legally and practicably available reproductive health services.

It is well known that those who develop policies and programs, or who provide services, are not the most objective judges of the value of what they do. As a result, outside evaluators, without an ax to grind, would need to be used. To increase the worth of the evaluation, the provision of funds for services would have to be contingent upon cooperation with outside evaluators; and procedures would have to be adopted to make sure that the evaluators are not co-opted by the service providers.

The implemented policies should be evaluated to determine their impact on the incidence of premarital sexual intercourse, use of contraception, unwanted pregnancy, abortion, adoption, and parent-child communication. For example, although lowering the age of consent to 15 for reproductive health services seems to be the most reasonable approach to take, the actual effects of instituting the policy would need to be carefully monitored. The results of a careful evaluation may suggest modifications. Perhaps the age of consent should be lowered to 14, or raised to 16, or restored to 18. Evaluating the results by age, over a period of several years, would help to decide such questions.

An example of modifying policies based upon the evaluation of results is provided by the legal age for drinking alcoholic beverages. After the ratification of the Twenty-Sixth Amendment, in 1971, more than half of the states lowered their legal drinking age. By 1975, evidence of negative consequences, especially increased automobile accidents by young people, reversed the trend, and many states raised the minimum drinking age (Wagenaar 1981). The potential for competence and responsibility among teenagers is clearly not uniform across all areas of behavior. Perhaps the ubiquity of the automobile for adolescents in the United States creates an especially hazardous situation out of teenage drinking. The point, of course, is that we should not cast our policies and programs in concrete, and should consider changes based on a continuous flow of evaluative information.

In short, the social science information currently available lends reasoned support to the three policy recommendations we have made. Whatever policies are adopted, however, the area of minors' sexual rights is too important to be left to the vagaries of chance or the controversies of clashing values. There is general awareness of the importance of the issue and of the substantial impact that government policies can have. There should therefore also be general agreement to evaluate the policies in this area, whatever they are, in order to examine their effects. If this is done, it is our belief that the general shape of government policy will gradually come to resemble what we are proposing.

Bibliography

ABC News/Washington Post Poll, 1981. Survey #0034, June 8.

Adelson, J. 1972. The political imagination of the young adolescent. In J. Kagan and R. Cole, eds. *Twelve to Sixteen: Early Adolescence,* pp. 106–143. New York: Norton.

AGI. 1976. *11 Million Teenagers.* New York: Alan Guttmacher Institute.

—— 1981. *Teenage Pregnancy: The Problem That Hasn't Gone Away.* New York: Alan Guttmacher Institute.

Allen, J. E. and D. Bender. 1980. *Managing Teenage Pregnancy: Access to Abortion, Contraception, and Sex Education.* New York: Praeger.

Alexander, S. J., C. D. Williams, and J. B. Forbush. 1980. *Overview of State Policies Related to Adolescent Parenthood.* Washington, D.C.: National Association of State Boards of Education.

ABA (American Bar Association). 1977. *Rights of Minors.* Cambridge, Mass.: Ballinger.

ALI/ABA (American Law Institute/American Bar Association). 1977. *Law and Tactics in Juvenile Cases.* 3d ed.

Badgley Report. 1977. *Report of the Committee on the Operation of the Abortion Law,* Robin F. Badgley, chairman. Ottawa, Canada: Minister of Supply and Services.

Baker, C. D. 1982. The adolescent as theorist: An interpretive view. *Journal of Youth and Adolescence* 11:167–182.

Baldwin, W. H. 1976. *Adolescent Pregnancy and Childbearing: Growing Concerns for Americans.* Population Bulletin vol. 31, no. 2. Washington, D.C.: Population Reference Bureau.

—— 1981. Adolescent pregnancy and childbearing: An overview. *Seminars in Perinatology* 5:1–8.

Bane, M. J. 1976. *Here to Stay: American Families in the Twentieth Century.* New York: Basic Books.

Baumrind, D. 1968. Authoritarian vs. authoritative parental control. *Adolescence* 13:255–272.

—— 1971. Current patterns of parental authority. *Developmental Psychology* 4:1–103.

—— 1973. The development of instrumental competence through socialization. In *Minnesota Symposia on Child Psychology* 7:3–46. Minneapolis: University of Minnesota Press.

—— 1975. The contributions of the family to the development of competence in children. *Schizophrenia Bulletin* 14:12–37.

—— 1978a. Parental disciplinary patterns and social competence in children. *Youth and Society* 9:239–275.

—— 1978b. Reciprocal rights and responsibilities in parent-child relations. *Journal of Social Issues* 34:179–196.

Bell, R. R. 1966. Parent-child conflict in sexual values. *Journal of Social Issues* 22:34–44.

Bennett, S. M. and W. B. Dickinson. 1980. Student-parent rapport and parent involvement in sex, birth control, and venereal disease education. *Journal of Sex Research* 16:114–130.

Berzonsky, M. D. 1978. Formal reasoning in adolescence: An alternative view. *Adolescence* 13:279–290.

Besharov, D. J. 1982. Representing abused and neglected children: When protecting children means seeking the dismissal of court proceedings. *Journal of Family Law* 20:217–239.

Blackstone, I. W. 1765. *Commentaries on the Laws of England.* Oxford: Clarendon Press.

Blalock, H. M. and P. H. Wilken. 1979. *Intergroup Processes: A Micro-Macro Perspective.* New York: Free Press.

Blake, J. and J. H. Del Pinal. 1981. Negativism, equivocation, and wobbly assent: Public "support" for the prochoice platform on abortion. *Demography* 18:309–320.

Blumer, H. 1969. *Symbolic Interactionism.* Englewood Cliffs, N.J.: Prentice-Hall.

Bolton, F. G. 1980. *The Pregnant Adolescent: Problems of Premature Parenthood.* Beverly Hills, Calif.: Sage Publications.

Bowerman, C. E. and J. W. Kinch. 1969. Changes in family and peer orientation of children between the fourth and tenth grades. In M. Gold and E. Douvan, eds., *Adolescent Development: Readings in Research and Theory,* pp. 137–146. Boston: Allyn and Bacon.

Boyd, E., J. Clark, H. Kempur, P. Johannet, B. Leonard, and P. McPherson. 1974. Teaching interpersonal communication to troubled families. *Family Process* 13:317–336.

Brittain, C. V. 1967. An exploration of bases of peer-compliance and parent-compliance in adolescence. *Adolescence* 2:445–448.

Bronfenbrenner, U. 1976. Who cares for America's children? In V. C. Vaughan, III, and T. B. Brazelton, eds., *The Family: Can It Be Saved?* pp. 3–32. Chicago: Year Book Medical Publishers.

—— 1977a. The calamitous decline of the American family. *Washington Post,* January 2, 1977, pp. C1, C3.

—— 1977b. Nobody home: The erosion of the American family (A conversation with Urie Bronfenbrenner). *Psychology Today* 10:41–47.

—— 1979. *The Ecology of Human Development: Experiments by Nature and Design.* Cambridge: Harvard University Press.

Bronson, W. C. 1974. Mother-toddler interaction: A perspective on studying the development of competence. *Merrill-Palmer Quarterly* 20:215–301.

Bullough, V. L. 1981. Age at menarche: A misunderstanding. *Science* 213:365–366.

Bush, D. 1983. Fertility-related state laws passed in 1982. *Family Planning Perspectives* 15:111–116.

Caldwell, B. 1980. Balancing children's rights and parents' rights. In R. Haskins and J. J. Gallagher, eds., *Care and Education of Young Children in America: Policy, Politics, and Social Science,* pp. 27–50. Norword, N.J.: Ablex.

Card, J. J. and L. L. Wise. 1978. Teenage mothers and teenage fathers: The impact of early childbearing on the parents' personal and professional lives. *Family Planning Perspectives* 10:199–205.

Catton, K. 1981. Children in the courts. In H. H. Irving, ed., *Family Law: An Interdisciplinary Perspective,* pp. 185–215. Toronto: Carswell.

Chamie, M., S. Eisman, J. D. Forrest, M. T. Orr, and A. Torres. 1982. Factors affecting adolescents' use of family planning clinics. *Family Planning Perspectives* 14:126–139.

Chamie, M. and S. K. Henshaw. 1981. The costs and benefits of government expenditures for family planning programs. *Family Planning Perspectives* 13:117–124.

Chand, I. P., D. M. Crider, and F. K. Willets. 1975. Parent-youth disagreement as perceived by youth. *Youth and Society* 6:365–376.

CDC (Centers for Disease Control). 1972. *Abortion Surveillance 1970.* Atlanta, Ga.

—— 1977. *Abortion Surveillance 1975.*

—— 1980. *Abortion Surveillance 1978.*

Chilman, C. S. 1978. *Adolescent Sexuality in a Changing American Society.* U.S. Department of Health, Education, and Welfare, Public Health Service, DHEW Publication No. (NIH) 79-1426.

—— 1980. Social and psychological research concerning adolescent childbearing: 1970–1980. *Journal of Marriage and the Family* 42:793–805.

Clarke-Stewart, A. 1977. *Child Care in the Family: A Review of Research and Some Propositions for Policy.* New York: Academic Press.

Clayton, R. R. and J. L . Bokemeier. 1980. Premarital sex in the seventies. *Journal of Marriage and the Family* 42:759–775.

Coleman, J. S. 1972. *Policy Research in the Social Sciences.* Morristown, N.J.: General Learning Press.

Condry, J. and M. L. Siman. 1974. Characteristics of peer- and adult-oriented children. *Journal of Marriage and the Family* 36:543–554.

CRS (Congressional Research Service). 1979. Not for adults alone: Children begin pressing for their constitutional rights. *Civil Rights Digest* 26:113–121.

Connolly, K. and J. Bruner. 1974. Competence: Its nature and nurture. In K. Connolly and J. Bruner, eds., *The Growth of Competence,* pp. 3–10. New York: Academic Press.

Conrad, D. and D. Hedin. 1982. The impact of experiential education on adolescent development. *Children and Youth Services* 4:57–76.

Constantine, L. L. 1977. Open family: A lifestyle for kids and other people. *Family Coordinator* 26:113–121.

Cutright, P. and F. S. Jaffe. 1977. *Impact of Family Planning Programs on Fertility: The U. S. Experience.* New York: Praeger.

DeLamater, J. and P. MacCorquodale. 1979. *Premarital Sexuality.* Madison: University of Wisconsin Press.

Dibble, E. and D. J. Cohen. 1974. Companion instruments for measuring children's competence and parental style. *Archives of General Psychiatry* 30:805–815.

Dickens, C. 1843. *The Life and Adventures of Martin Chuzzlewitt.* London: Chapman and Hall.

Donovan, P. 1981. Your parents or the judge: Massachusetts' new abortion consent law. *Family Planning Perspectives* 13:224–228.

—— 1982a. Fertility-related state laws enacted in 1981. *Family Planning Perspectives* 14:63–67.

—— 1982b. Airing contraceptive commercials. *Family Planning Perspectives* 14:321–324.

Dryfoos, J. and N. Bourque-Scholl. 1981. *Factbook on Teenage Pregnancy.* New York: Alan Guttmacher Institute.

Dubbe, M. C. 1965. What parents are not told may hurt: A study of communication between teenagers and parents. *Family Life Coordinator* 14:51–118.

Dworkin, R. J. and A. N. Poindexter. 1980. Pregnant low-income teenagers: A social structural model of the determinants of abortion-seeking behavior. *Youth and Society* 11:295–309.

Edelman, P. B. 1973. The Massachusetts task force reports: Advocacy for children. *Harvard Educational Review* 13:639–652.

Edwards, L. E., M. E. Steinman, K. A. Arnold, and E. Y. Hakanson. 1980. Adolescent pregnancy prevention services in high school clinics. *Family Planning Perspectives* 12:6–14.

Elder, G. H. 1962. Structural variations in the child rearing relationship. *Sociometry* 25:241–262.

—— 1963. Parental power legitimation and its effect on the adolescent. *Sociometry* 26:50–65.

Elkind, D. 1967a. Cognitive structure and adolescent experience. *Adolescence* 2:427–434.

—— 1967b. Egocentrism in adolescence. *Child Development* 38:1025–1034.

—— 1974. *Children and Adolescents.* New York: Oxford University Press.

—— 1978. Understanding the young adolescent. *Adolescence* 13:127–134.

Ellsworth, P. C. and R. J. Levy. 1969–70. Legislative reform of child custody adjudication: An effort to rely on social science data in formulating legal policies. *Law and Society Review* 4:166–225.

Emerson, T. I. 1963. Toward a general theory of the first amendment. *Yale Law Review* 72:877–956.

Emmerich, H. J. 1978. The influence of parents and peers on choices made by adolescents. *Journal of Youth and Adolescence* 7:175–180.

Enright, R. D. 1976. Social cognition in children: A model for intervention. *The Counseling Psychologist* 6:65–70.

Enright, R. D., D. K. Lapsley, A. E. Drivas, and L. A. Fehr. 1980. Parental influence on the development of adolescent autonomy and identity. *Journal of Youth and Adolescence* 9:529–545.

Erickson, F. and J. Schultz. 1977. When is a context? Some issues and methods in the analysis of social competence. *Quarterly Newsletter of the Institute for Comparative Human Development* (Rockefeller University) 1:5–10.

FLR. 1983. Runaway's parents must return to the United States to get custody back. *Family Law Reporter* 9:2499–2500.

Farson, R. 1974. *Birthrights*. New York: Macmillan.

Faught, J. 1980. Presuppositions of the Chicago School in the work of Everett C. Hughes. *American Sociologist* 15:72–82.

Feshbach, N. and C. Tremper. 1981. Attitudes of parents and adolescents toward decision making by minors. Paper presented at American Psychological Association Annual Meeting, August 1981, Los Angeles.

Finkel, M. L. and D. J. Finkel. 1978. Male adolescent contraceptive utilization. *Adolescence* 13:443–451.

Finkelhor, D. 1979. What's wrong with sex between adults and children? Ethics and the problem of sexual abuse. *American Journal of Orthopsychiatry* 49:692–697.

Fitzgerald, J. M., J. R. Nesselroade, and P. B. Baltes. 1973. Emergence of adult intellectual structure: Prior to or during adolescence? *Developmental Psychology* 9:114–119.

Foote, N. N. and L. S. Cottrell, Jr. 1955. *Identity and Interpersonal Competence: A New Direction in Family Research*. Chicago: University of Chicago Press.

Forman, S. G. and B. D. Forman. 1981. Family environment and its relation to adolescent personality factors. *Journal of Personality Assessment* 45:163–167.

Forrest, J. D., A. I. Hermalin, and S. K. Henshaw. 1981. The impact of family planning clinic programs on adolescent pregnancy. *Family Planning Perspectives* 13:109–116.

Fost, N. 1976. Ethical problems in pediatrics. *Current Problems in Pediatrics* 6:3–31.

Foster, H., Jr. and D. Freed. 1972. A bill of rights for children. *Family Law Quarterly* 6:343–375.

Fox, G. L. 1977. "Nice girl": Social control of women through a value construct. *Signs* 2:805–817.

—— 1979. *Mothers and Their Teenaged Daughters: A Report to the Participants in the Mother-Daughter Communication Project*. Mimeographed.

—— 1981. The family's role in adolescent sexual behavior. In T. Ooms, ed., *Teenage Pregnancy in a Family Context*, pp. 73–130. Philadelphia: Temple University Press.

Fox, G. L. and J. K. Inazu. 1980a. Patterns and outcomes of mother-daughter communication about sexuality. *Journal of Social Issues* 36:7–29.

—— 1980b. Mother-daughter communication about sex. *Family Relations* 29:347–352.

Freeman, E. W. and K. Rickels. 1979. Adolescent contraceptive use: Current status of practice and research. *Obstetrics and Gynecology* 53:388–394.

Furstenberg, F. F., Jr. 1976. *Unplanned Parenthood: The Social Consequences of Teenage Childbearing*. New York: Free Press.

Furstenberg, F. F., Jr., R. Herceg-Baron, D. Mann, and J. Shaw. 1982. Parental involvement: Selling family planning clinics short. *Family Planning Perspectives* 14:140–144.

GOI (Gallup Opinion Index), Report 156, July 1978.

GYS (Gallup Youth Survey). 1978. Associated Press Release, October 11, 1978.

Gaylin, N. L. 1981. Family life education: Behavioral science wonderbread? *Family Relations* 30:511–516.

Gaylin, W. 1982. The competence of children: No longer all or none. *The Hastings Center Report* 12:33–38.

Gebhard, P. H. 1977. The acquisition of basic sex information. *Journal of Sex Research* 13:148–169.

General Mills. 1977. *The General Mills American Family Report.* Conducted by Yankelovich, Skelly, and White, Inc. Minneapolis: General Mills, Inc.

—— 1979. *American Family Report 1978–1979: Family Health in an Era of Stress.* Conducted by Yankelovich, Skelly and White, Inc. Minneapolis: General Mills, Inc.

Goldstein, J., A. Freud, and A. J. Solnit. 1979. *Beyond the Best Interest of the Child.* New York: Free Press.

Goodman, N. 1969. Adolescent norms and behavior: Organization and conformity. *Merrill-Palmer Quarterly* 15:199–211.

Goodman, B. and N. Goodman. 1976. Effects of parent orientation meetings on parent-child communication about sexuality and family life. *Family Coordinator* 25:285–290.

Gordon, S. 1981. The case for a moral sex education in the schools. *Journal of School Health* 51:214–218.

Gough, A. R. and M. Grilli. 1973. The unruly child and the law: Toward a focus on the family. *Juvenile Justice* 23:9–12.

Granberg, D. and B. W. Granberg. 1980. Abortion attitudes, 1965–1980: Trends and determinants. *Family Planning Perspectives* 12:250–261.

Green, C. P. and K. Poteteiger. 1978. Teenage pregnancy: A major problem for minors. *Society* 15:8–13.

Grisso, T. and L. Vierling. 1978. Minors' consent to treatment: A developmental perspective. *Professional Psychology* 9:412–427.

Gross, B. and R. Gross, eds. 1977. *The Children's Rights Movement: Overcoming the Oppression of Young People.* Garden City, N.Y.: Anchor/Doubleday.

Gunter, N. C. and R. C. LaBarba. 1981. Maternal and perinatal effects of adolescent childbearing. *International Journal of Behavioral Development* 4:333–357.

Hafen, B. C. 1977. Puberty, privacy and protection: The risks of children's rights. *American Bar Association Journal* 63:1383–1388.

Harman, D. and O. G. Brim, Jr. 1980. *Learning to be Parents: Principles, Programs, and Methods.* Beverly Hills, Calif.: Sage.

HLJ (Hastings Law Journal). 1967. Child vs. parent: Erosion of the immunity rule. *Hastings Law Journal* 19:201–222.

Heath, D. H. 1977. *Maturity and Competence.* New York: Gardner Press.

Henshaw, S. K., J. D. Forrest, E. Sullivan, and C. Tietze. 1982. Abortion services in the United States, 1979 and 1980. *Family Planning Perspectives* 14:5–15.

Henshaw, S. K. and K. O'Reilly. 1983. Characteristics of abortion patients in the United States, 1979 and 1980. *Family Planning Perspectives* 15:5–16.

Herceg-Baron, R. and F. F. Furstenberg, Jr. 1982. Adolescent contraceptive use: The impact of family support systems. In G. L. Fox, ed., *The Childbearing Decision: Fertility Attitudes and Behavior,* pp. 125–143. Beverly Hills, Calif.: Sage.

Herold, E. S. 1981. Contraceptive embarrassment and contraceptive behavior among young single women. *Journal of Youth and Adolescence* 10:233–242.

Hess, R. D. 1974. Social competence and the educational process. In K. Connolly and J. Bruner, eds., *The Growth of Competence,* pp. 283–302. New York: Academic Press.

Hobbs, N. and S. Robinson. 1982. Adolescent development and public policy. *American Psychologist* 37:212–223.

Howard, A. 1982. Interactional psychology: Some implications for psychological anthropology. *American Anthropologist* 84:37–57.

Inazu, J. K. and G. L. Fox. 1980. Maternal influence on the sexual behavior of teenage daughters. *Journal of Family Issues* 1:81–102.

Inkeles, A. 1966. Social structure and the socialization of competence. *Harvard Educational Review* 36:265–283.

IJA (Institute of Judicial Administration and American Bar Association). 1980. *Standards Relating to Rights of Minors.* Cambridge, Mass.: Ballinger.

Jessor, S. L. and R. Jessor. 1974. Maternal ideology and adolescent problem behavior. *Developmental Psychology* 10:246–254.

Johnson, J. H. 1982. Abortion and women's health: A meeting of the National Abortion Federation. *Family Planning Perspectives* 14:327–328.

Jones, E. F., J. R. Beninger, and C. F. Westoff. 1980. Pill and IUD discontinuation in the United States, 1970–1975: The influence of the media. *Family Planning Perspectives* 12:293–300.

Kagan, J. 1972. A conception of early adolescence. In J. Kagan and R. Coles, eds., *Twelve to Sixteen: Early Adolescence,* pp. 90–105. New York: Norton.

Kasun, J. R. 1978. Teenage pregnancy: A reply to zero population growth. *Society* 15:9–15.

Katz, S. N., W. A. Schroeder, and L. R. Sidman. 1973. Emancipating our children: Coming of legal age in America. *Family Law Quarterly* 7:211–241.

Kenney, A. M., J. D. Forrest, and A. Torres. 1982. Storm over Washington: The parental notification proposal. *Family Planning Perspectives* 14:185–197.

Kilmann, P. R., R. L. Wanlass, R. F. Sabalis, and B. Sullivan. 1981. Sex education: A review of its effects. *Archives of Sexual Behavior* 10:177–205.

Kirby, D., J. Alter, and P. Scales. 1979. *An Analysis of U.S. Sex Education Programs and Evaluation Methods.* Springfield, Va.: National Technical Information Service.

Koenig, M. A. and M. Zelnik. 1982. The risk of premarital first pregnancy among metropolitan-area teenagers: 1976 and 1979. *Family Planning Perspectives* 14:239–247.

Kovar, L. C. 1968. *Faces of the Adolescent Girl.* Englewood Cliffs, N.J.: Prentice-Hall.

Kurtines, W. 1978. A measure of autonomy. *Journal of Personality Assessment* 42:253–257.

Lambert, B. F., B. Rothschild, R. Altland, and L. B. Green. 1972. *Adolescence: Transition from Childhood to Maturity.* Monterey, Calif.: Brooks/Cole.

Lange, G., G. Ladd, and A. Davis. 1982. Parents, teachers, and competent children. Paper presented at the Annual Meetings of the Midwestern Association for the Education of Young Children, Indianapolis, May.

Larson, L. E. 1972. The influence of parents and peers during adolescence: The situation hypothesis revisited. *Journal of Marriage and Family* 34:67–74.

—— 1974. An examination of the salience hierarchy during adolescence: The influence of the family. *Adolescence* 9:317–332.

Lasch, C. 1975. *Haven in a Heartless World: The Family Besieged*. New York: Basic Books.

Laws, J. L. and P. Schwartz. 1977. *Sexual Scripts: The Social Construction of Female Sexuality*. Hinsdale, Ill.: Dryden Press.

Lee, J. A. 1982. Three paradigms of childhood. *Canadian Review of Sociology and Anthropology* 19:591–608.

Levy, R. J. 1977. The rights of parents. In B. A. Chadwick, ed., *Government Impact on Family Life*, pp. 41–55. Provo, Utah: Brigham Young University Press.

Lewis, C. 1981. How adolescents approach decisions: Changes over grades seven to twelve and policy implications. *Child Development* 52:538–544.

Lucretius, T. (Written between 94 and 55 B.C.) *De Rerum Natura*.

Luker, K. 1975. *Taking Chances: Abortion and the Decision Not to Contracept*. Berkeley: University of California Press.

McAnarney, E. R. and H . A. Thiede. 1981. Adolescent pregnancy and childbearing: What we have learned in a decade and what remains to be learned. *Seminars in Perinatology* 5:91–103.

McClelland, D. C., C. A. Constantian, D. Regalado, and C. Stone. 1978. Making it to maturity. *Psychology Today* 12:42–53, 114.

McCurdy, W. E. 1930. Torts between persons in domestic relations. *Harvard Law Review* 43:1030–1082.

MacIntyre, S. 1977. *Single and Pregnant*. London: Croom Helm.

McKenry, P. C., L. H. Walters, and C. Johnson. 1979. Adolescent pregnancy: A review of the literature. *Family Coordinator* 28:17–28.

McMurty, J. 1979–80. The case for children's liberation. *Interchange* 10:10–37.

Magnusson, D. and N. S. Endler, eds. 1977. *Personality at the Crossroads: Current Issues in Interactional Psychology*. Hillsdale, N.J.: Lawrence Erlbaum Associates.

Manaster, S. J. 1977. *Adolescent Development and the Life Task*. Boston: Allyn and Bacon.

Marks, G. 1975. Detours on the road to maturity: A view of the legal conception of growing up and letting go. *Law and Contemporary Problems* 39:78–92.

Marsh, D. T., F. C. Serafica, and C. Barenboim. 1980. Effects of perspective-taking training on interpersonal problem solving. *Child Development* 51:140–145.

Mayer, J. 1982. Viewers' objections may block TV ads for contraceptives. *Wall Street Journal*, January 21, 1982.

Meltzer, B. N. and J. G. Manis, eds. 1978. *Symbolic Interaction: A Reader in Social Psychology*. 3d ed. Boston: Allyn and Bacon.

Midonick, M. 1972. *Children, Parents, and the Courts: Juvenile Delinquency, Ungovernability, and Neglect*. New York: Practicing Law Institute.

Miller, D. 1974. *Adolescence: Psychology, Psychopathology, and Psychotherapy*. New York: J. Aronson.

Miller, M. J. 1975. Adolescence and authority. In S. Meyerson, ed., *Adolescence: The Crises of Adjustment*, pp. 73–89. London: Allen and Unwin.

MLR. 1977. Note. *Missouri Law Review* 42:291–297.

Mnookin, R. H. 1978a. *Child, Family, and State: Problems and Materials on Children and the Law*. Boston: Little, Brown.

—— 1978b. Children's rights: Beyond kiddie libbers and child savers. *Journal of Clinical Child Psychology* 7:163–167.

Moore, K. A., S. L. Hofferth, R. F. Wertheimer, L. J. Waite, and S. B. Caldwell. 1981. Teenage childbearing: Consequences for women, families, and government welfare expenditures. In K. G. Scott, T. Field, and E. G. Robertson, eds., *Teenage Parents and Their Offspring*, pp. 35–54. New York: Grune and Stratton.

Mosteller, F. 1981. Taking science out of social science. *Science* 212:291.

Moynihan, D. P. 1979. Social science and the courts. *Public Interest* 54:12–31.

Murray, J. E., Jr. 1974. *Law of Contracts*. Indianapolis: Bobbs-Merrill.

Mussen, P. H., J. J. Conger, and J. Kagan. 1969. *Child Development and Personality*. 3d ed. New York: Harper and Row.

Muuss, R. E. 1982. Social cognition: Robert Selman's theory of role taking. *Adolescence* 17:499–526.

Nye, F. I. 1976. *School-Age Parenthood: Consequences for Babies, Mothers, Fathers, Grandparents, and Others*. Washington State University Cooperative Extension Service, Bulletin 667.

Okada, L. M. and D. G. Gillespie. 1977. The impact of family planning programs on unplanned pregnancies. *Family Planning Perspectives* 9:173–176.

Ooms, T. 1981. Family involvement, notification, and responsibility. In T. Ooms, ed., *Teenage Pregnancy in a Family Context*, pp. 371–398. Philadelphia: Temple University Press.

Orr, M. T. 1982. Sex education and contraceptive education in U.S. public high schools. *Family Planning Perspectives* 14:304–313.

Oskamp, S. and B. Mindick. 1983. Personality and attitudinal barriers to contraception. In D. Byrne and W. A. Fisher, eds., *Adolescents, Sex and Contraception* pp. 65–107. Hillsdale, N.J.: Lawrence Erlbaum Associates.

Paul, E. W. 1977. Danforth and Bellotti: A breakthrough for adolescents. *Family Planning/Population Reporter* 6:3–5.

Paul, E. W. and H. F. Pilpel. 1979. Teenagers and pregnancy: The law in 1979. *Family Planning Perspectives* 11:297–302.

Paul, E. W. and G. Scofield. 1979. Informed consent for fertility control services. *Family Planning Perspectives* 11:159–168.

Peel, E. A. 1971. *The Nature of Adolescent Judgment*. New York: Wiley Interscience.

—— 1975. Predilection for generalizing and abstracting. *British Journal of Educational Psychology* 45:177–188.

Peterson, D. R. 1977. A functional approach to the study of person-person interactions. In D. Magnusson and N. S. Endler, eds., *Personality at the Crossroads: Current Issues in Interactional Psychology*, pp. 305–316. Hillsdale, N.J.: Lawrence Erlbaum Associates.

Phipps-Yonas, S. 1980. Teenage pregnancy and motherhood: A review of the literature. *American Journal of Orthopsychiatry* 50:403–431.

Piaget, J. 1972. Intellectual evolution from adolescence to adulthood. *Human Development* 15:1–12.

Pilpel, H. F. and L. R. Rockett. 1981. Sex education and the law. In L. Brown, ed., *Sex Education in the Eighties*, pp. 19–29. New York: Plenum Press.

Presser, H. B. 1974. Early motherhood: Ignorance or bliss? *Family Planning Perspectives* 6:8–14.

—— 1977. Guessing and misinformation about pregnancy risk among urban mothers. *Family Planning Perspectives* 9:111–115.

Prewitt, K. 1980. Social science utilities. *Society* 17:6–8.

Prosser, W. 1971. *The Law of Torts*. 4th ed. St. Paul: West.

Rains, P. 1971. *Becoming an Unwed Mother*. Chicago: Aldine-Atherton.

Rausch, H. L. 1977. Paradox, levels, and junctures in person-situation systems. In D. Magnusson and N. S. Endler, eds., *Personality at the Crossroads: Current Issues in Interactional Psychology*, pp. 287–304. Hillsdale, N.J.: Lawrence Erlbaum Associates.

Reisman, J. 1980. Nice girl imagery and teenagers' decision to abort: A study of middle-class teenagers' reactions to pregnancy. Paper presented at American Sociological Association Annual Meeting, August 28, 1980, New York.

Reiss, I. L. 1980. *Family Systems in America*. 3d ed. New York: Holt, Rinehart, and Winston.

Reiss, I. L. and B. C. Miller. 1979. Heterosexual permissiveness: A theoretical analysis. In W. R. Burr, R. Hill, F. I. Nye, and I. L. Reiss, eds., *Contemporary Theories About the Family*, pp. 57–100. New York: Free Press.

Rice, F. P. 1975. *The Adolescent: Development, Relationships, and Culture*. Boston: Allyn and Bacon.

Roberts, E. J., D. Kline, and J. Gagnon. 1978. *Family Life and Sexual Learning: A Study of the Role of Parents in the Sexual Learning of Children*, vol. 1. Cambridge, Mass.: Population Education.

Roberts, E. J. 1980. Sex education versus sexual learning. In M. Kirkpatrick, ed., *Women's Sexual Development: Explorations of Inner Space*, pp. 239–250. New York: Plenum Press.

Rodman, H. 1970. *Teaching About Families: Textbook Evaluations and Recommendations for Secondary Schools*. Cambridge, Mass.: Howard A. Doyle.

—— 1971. *Lower-Class Families*. New York: Oxford University Press.

—— 1981. Future directions for abortion morality and policy. In P. Sachdev, ed., *Abortion: Readings and Research*, pp. 229–237. Toronto: Butterworths.

Rollins, B. C. and D. L. Thomas. 1979. Parental support, power, and control techniques in the socialization of children. In W. Burr, R. Hill, I. Nye, and I. L. Reiss, eds., *Contemporary Theories About the Family*, 1:317–364. New York: Free Press.

Rosen, R. H. 1980. Adolescent pregnancy decision making: Are parents important? *Adolescence* 15:43–54.

—— 1982. Pregnancy resolution decisions: A review and appraisal of research. In G. L. Fox, ed., *The Childbearing Decision: Fertility Attitudes and Behavior*, pp. 247–266. Beverly Hills, Calif.: Sage.

Rothchild, E. 1979. Female power: Lines to development of autonomy in adolescent girls. In M. Sugar, ed., *Female Adolescent Development*, pp. 274–295. New York: Brunner/Mazel.

Sarvis, B. and H. Rodman. 1974. *The Abortion Controversy*. 2d ed. New York: Columbia University Press.

Satir, V. M. 1972. *Peoplemaking*. Palo Alto, Calif.: Science and Behavior Books.

Scales, P. 1981. Sex education in the '70s and '80s: Accomplishments, obstacles, and emerging issues. *Family Relations* 30:557–566.

Scanzoni, J. 1983. *Shaping Tomorrow's Family: Theory and Policy for the 21st Century*. Beverly Hills, Calif.: Sage.

Scanzoni, J. and M. Szinovacz. 1980. *Family Decision Making: A Developmental Sex Role Model*. Beverly Hills, Calif.: Sage.

Schelling, T. C. 1971. On the ecology of micromotives. *The Public Interest* Fall:61–98.

Schinke, S. P., B. J. Blythe, and L . D. Gilchrist. 1981. Cognitive-behavioral prevention of adolescent pregnancy. *Journal of Counseling Psychology* 28:451–454.

Scott, R. A. and A. R. Shore. 1979. *Why Sociology Does Not Apply*. New York: Elsevier.

Sears, R., E. E. Maccoby, and H. Levin. 1957. *Patterns of Child Raaring*. Evanston, Ill.: Row, Peterson.

SP (Select Panel for the Promotion of Child Health). 1981. *Better Health for Our Children: A National Strategy*. Report to the U.S. Congress and the Secretary of Health and Human Services, vol. 1. Washington, D.C.: Department of Health and Human Services.

Shah, F., M. Zelnik, and J. F. Kantner. 1975. Unprotected intercourse among unwed teenagers. *Family Planning Perspectives* 7:39–44.

Sharpe, L. J. 1977. The social scientist and policy making: Some cautionary thoughts and transatlantic reflections. In C. Weiss, ed., *Using Social Research in Public Policy Making*, pp. 37–54. Lexington, Mass.: Lexington Books.

Shears, C. C. 1962. Legal problems peculiar to children's courts. *American Bar Association Journal* 48:719–724.

Silber, T. J. 1980. Values relating to abortion as expressed by the inner city adolescent girl: Report of a physician's experience. *Adolescence* 15:183–189.

Skegg, P. G. 1971. Consent to medical procedures on minors. *Modern Law Review* 36:370–381.

Smith, M. B. 1968. Toward a conception of the competent self. In J. A. Clausen, ed., *Socialization and Society*, pp. 270–320. Boston: Little, Brown.

Smith, T. E. 1971. Birth order, sibship size, and social class as antecedents of adolescents' acceptance of parents' authority. *Social Forces* 50:223–231.

—— 1977. An empirical comparison of potential determinants of parental authority. *Journal of Marriage and the Family* 39:153–164.

Steiner, G. Y. 1976. *The Children's Cause*. Washington, D.C.: Brookings.

—— 1981. *The Futility of Family Policy*. Washington, D.C.: Brookings.

Steinfels, M. O. 1981. Ethical and legal issues in teenage pregnancies. In T. Ooms, ed., *Teenage Pregnancies in a Family Context*, pp. 277–306. Philadelphia: Temple University Press.

Stier, S. 1978. Children's rights and society's duties. *Journal of Social Issues* 34:46–58.

Stern, D., S. Smith, and F. Doolittle. 1975. How children used to work. *Law and Contemporary Problems* 39:93–117.

Stone, L. J. and J. Church. 1979. *Childhood and Adolescence: A Psychology of the Growing Person*. 4th ed. New York: Random House.

Straus, M., R. J. Gelles, and S. K. Steinmetz. 1980. *Behind Closed Doors: Violence in the American Family*. Garden City, N.Y.: Anchor Press/Doubleday.

Strauss, A. 1978. *Negotiations: Varieties, Contexts, Processes, and Social Order*. San Francisco: Jossey-Bass.

Sundquist, J. L. 1978. Research brokerage: The weak link. In L. E. Lynn, Jr., ed., *Knowledge and Policy: The Uncertain Connection*, pp. 126–144. Washington, D.C.: National Academy of Sciences.

Tanner, J. M. 1981. Menarcheal age (letter). *Science* 214:604.

Time. 1981a. Cradle-to-grave intimacy. September 7, 1981, p. 69.

—— 1981b. Age of accountability: When do juveniles become adults? December 14, 1981, p. 80.

Torres, A. 1978. Does your mother know . . . ? *Family Planning Perspectives* 10:280–282.

—— 1979. Rural and urban family planning services in the United States. *Family Planning Perspectives* 11:109–114.

Torres, A., J. D. Forrest, and S. Eisman. 1980. Telling parents: Clinic policies and adolescents' use of family planning and abortion services. *Family Planning Perspectives* 12:284–292.

Tribe, L. H. 1975. Childhood, suspect classifications, and conclusive presumptions: Three linked riddles. *Law and Contemporary Problems* 39:8–14.

Udry, J. R. and R. L. Cliquet. 1982. A cross-cultural examination of the relationship between ages at menarche, marriage, and first birth. *Demography* 19:53–63.

Utech, D. A. and K. L. Hoving. 1969. Parents and peers as competing influences in the decision of children of differing ages. *Journal of Social Psychology* 78:267–274.

Wagenaar, A. C. 1981. Effects of an increase in the legal minimum drinking age. *Journal of Public Health Policy* 2:206–225.

Wagner, C. A. 1980. Sexuality of American adolescents. *Adolescence* 15:567–580.

Wald, M. 1976. Legal policies affecting children: A lawyer's request for aid. *Child Development* 47:1–5.

Walters, J. and L. H. Walters. 1980. Parent-child relationships: A review, 1970–1979. *Journal of Marriage and the Family* 42:807–822.

Washington Memo, Planned Parenthood-World Population. 1981. Alan Guttmacher Institute, July 17.

Weithorn, L. A. and S. B. Campbell. 1982. The competency of children and adolescents to make informed treatment decisions. *Child Development* 53:1589–1598.

Westoff, C. F. and N. B. Ryder. 1977. *The Contraceptive Revolution.* Princeton, N.J.: Princeton University Press.

Wiley, N. 1979. The rise and fall of dominating theories in American sociology. In W. E. Snizek, E. R. Fuhrman, and M. K. Miller, eds., *Contemporary Issues in Theory and Research,* pp. 53–80. Westport, Conn.: Greenwood Press.

Wollfil, J. D. 1977. Changes in interpersonal communication patterns as a consequence of need of information. *Communication Research* 4:235–257.

Wyshak, G. and R. E. Frisch. Evidence for a secular trend in age of menarche. *New England Journal of Medicine* 306:1033–1035.

Young, L. R. 1954. *Out of Wedlock.* New York: McGraw-Hill.

Yudin, L. W. 1966. Formal thought in adolescence as a function of intelligence. *Child Development* 37:697–708.

Zabin, L. S. 1981. The impact of early use of prescription contraceptives on reducing premarital teenage pregnancies. *Family Planning Perspectives* 13:72–74.

Zabin, L. S. and S. D. Clark, Jr. 1981. Why they delay: A study of teenage family planning clinic patients. *Family Planning Perspectives* 13:205–217.

—— 1983. Institutional factors affecting teenagers' choice and reasons for delay in attending a family planning clinic. *Family Planning Perspectives* 15:25–29.

Zabin, L. S., J. F. Kantner, and M. Zelnik. 1979. The risk of adolescent pregnancy in the first months of intercourse. *Family Planning Perspectives* 11:215–222.

Zelnik, M. 1979. Sex education and knowledge of pregnancy risk among U.S. teenage women. *Family Planning Perspectives* 11:355–357.

Zelnik, M. and J. F. Kantner. 1977. Sexual and contraceptive experience of young unmarried women in the United States, 1976 and 1971. *Family Planning Perspectives* 9:55–71.

—— 1978. First pregnancies to women aged 15–19: 1976 and 1971. *Family Planning Perspectives* 10:11–20.

—— 1979. Reasons for nonuse of contraception by sexually active women aged 15–19. *Family Planning Perspectives* 11:289–296.

—— 1980. Sexual activity, contraceptive use and pregnancy among metropolitan-area teenagers: 1971–1979. *Family Planning Perspectives* 12:230–237.

Zelnik, M., J. F. Kantner, and K. Ford. 1981. *Sex and Pregnancy in Adolescence.* Beverly Hills, Calif.: Sage.

Zelnik, M. and Y. J. Kim. 1982. Sex education and its association with teenage sexual activity, pregnancy and contraceptive use. *Family Planning Perspectives* 14:117–126.

Zelnik, M., Y. J. Kim, and J. F. Kantner. 1979. Probabilities of intercourse and conception among U.S. teenage women, 1971 and 1976. *Family Planning Perspectives* 11:177–183.

Zelnik, M. and F. K. Shah. 1983. First intercourse among young Americans. *Family Planning Perspectives* 15:64–70.

Cases, Statutes, and Restatements

Akron vs. Akron Center for Reproductive Health et al., U.S. Supreme Court, Nos. 81-746 and 81-1172 (June 15, 1983).
Baker vs. Bolton, 1808, 1 Camp. 493, 1970 Eng. Rep. 1033.
Bellotti vs. Baird, 428 U.S. 132 (1976).
Bellotti vs. Baird, 443 U.S. 622 (1979).
California Civil Code No. 64. Amended in 1979 and currently in effect.
Carey vs. Population Services International, 431 U.S. 678 (1977).
Doe vs. Irwin, 615 F.2d 1162 (6th Cir. 1980), *cert. denied*, 449 U.S. 829 (1980).
Eisenstadt vs. Baird, 405 U.S. 438 (1972).
Ellis vs. Dangelo, 116 Cal. App. 2d 30, 253 P.2d 675 (1953).
Ginsberg vs. New York, 390 U.S. 629 (1968).
Goss vs. Lopez, 419 U.S. 565 (1975).
Griswold vs. Connecticut, 381 U.S. 479 (1965).
Harris vs. McRae, 448 U.S. 297 (1980).
Hewelette vs. George, 68 Miss. 703, 9 So. 885 (1891).
H. L. vs. Matheson, 450 U.S. 398 (1981).
Holodook vs. Spencer, 36 N.Y.2d 35, 364 N.Y.S. 2d 859 (1974).
In the Matter of the Welfare of L.A.G. Hennapin County District Court (Juvenile Division), Minnesota, August 11, 1972. In H. Krause, *Cases and Materials on Family Law*. St. Paul: West, 1976.
In re Gault, 387 U.S. 1 (1967).
Kent vs. United States, 383 U.S. 541 (1966).
Keser vs. Chagnon, 159 Colo. 209, 410 P.2d 637 (1966).
Kilgrow vs. Kilgrow, 268 Ala. 275, 107 So. 2d 885 (1959).
Lassiter vs. Department of Social Services, 453 U.S. 18 (1981).
May vs. Anderson, 345 U.S. 528 (1953).
McKeiver vs. Pennsylvania, 403 U.S. 528 (1971).

Meyer vs. Nebraska, 262 U.S. 390 (1923).
Parham vs. J. R. and J. L., Minors, 442 U.S. 584, June (1979).
People ex rel. Sisson vs. Sisson, 271 N.Y. 285, 2 N.S. 2d 660 (1936).
Pierce vs. Society of Sisters, 268 U.S. 510 (1925).
Planned Parenthood of Central Missouri vs. Danforth, 428 U.S. 52 (1976).
Prince vs. Massachusetts, 321 U.S. 158 (1944).
Restatement (Second) of Torts, Sec. 316 (1965).
Restatement (Second) of Contracts, Sec. 18B (1975).
Roe vs. Wade, 410 U.S. 113 (1973).
Skinner vs. Oklahoma, 316 U.S. 535 (1942).
Tinker vs. Des Moines School District, 393 U.S. 503 (1969).
Watson vs. Kemp, 59 N.Y.S. 142 (1899).
West Virginia vs. Barnette, 319 U.S. 624 (1943).
Williamson vs. Garland, 402 S.W. 2d 80 (Ky. 1966).
Wycko vs. Gnodtke, 331 Mich. 331, 105 N.W.2d 118 (1960).

Cases, Statutes, and Restatements Index

Author Index

General Index